BLEU
1

McDOUGAL LITTELL

Discovering FRENCH
Nouveau!

Unit 5 Resource Book

Components authored by Jean-Paul Valette and Rebecca M. Valette:

- Workbook
- Communipak
- Assessment Program
- Video Program
- Audio Program

Components authored by Sloane Publications:

- Family Letter, *Patricia Smith*
- Absent Student Copymasters, *E. Kristina Baer*
- Family Involvement, *Patricia Smith*
- Multiple Choice Test Items, *Nicole Dicop-Hineline*

Other Components

- Video Activities, *T. Jeffrey Richards, Philip D. Korfe, Consultant*
- Comprehensive (Semester) Tests, *T. Jeffrey Richards*
- Activités pour tous, *Patricia L. Ménard*

ISBN: 0 - 618 - 29830 - 4

2 3 4 5 6 7 8 9 — MDO — 07 06 05 04 03

Table of Contents
Unité 5. En ville

URB
p. iii

LEÇON 16   Mes voisins   103

To the Teacher

The Unit Resource Books that accompany each unit of *Discovering French, Nouveau!–Bleu* provide a wide variety of materials to practice, expand on, and assess the material in the *Discovering French, Nouveau!–Bleu* student text.

Components

Following is a list of components included in each Unit Resource Book, correlated to each **Leçon:**
- Workbook, Teacher's Edition
- *Activités pour tous*, Teacher's Edition
- Lesson Plans
- Block Scheduling Lesson Plans
- Family Letter
- Absent Student Copymasters
- Family Involvement
- Video Activities
- Videoscripts
- Audioscripts
- Lesson Quizzes

Unit Resources include the following materials:
- Communipak
- *Activités pour tous* Reading, Teacher's Edition
- Workbook Reading and Culture Activities, Teacher's Edition
    Lesson Plans for *Images*
    Block Scheduling Lesson Plans for *Images*
- Assessment
    Unit Test
    Listening Comprehension Performance Test
    Speaking Performance Test
    Reading Comprehension Performance Test
    Writing Performance Test
    Multiple Choice Test Items
    Comprehensive Test
    Test Scoring Tools

- Audioscripts
- Answer Key

Component Description

Workbook, Teacher's Edition

The *Discovering French, Nouveau!–Bleu* Workbook directly references the student text. It provides additional practice to allow students to build their control of French and develop French proficiency. The activities provide guided communicative practice in meaningful contexts and frequent opportunity for self-expression.

Listening Activities give students the opportunity to demonstrate comprehension of spoken French in a variety of realistic contexts. Students listen to excerpts from the CD that accompanies the *Discovering French, Nouveau!–Bleu* program while working through listening activities to improve both general and discrete comprehension skills.

Writing Activities give students the chance to develop their writing skills and put into practice what they have learned in class. The last activity is called *Communication* and encourages students to express themselves in various additional communicative situations.

The Reading and Culture Activities contain realia (illustrations and objects from real life) from French-speaking countries and various kinds of cultural activities. Each unit includes one set of Reading and Culture Activities.

Activités pour tous, Teacher's Edition

The activities in *Activités pour tous* include vocabulary, grammar, and reading practice at varying levels of difficulty. Each practice section is three pages long, with each page corresponding to a level of difficulty (A, B, and C). A is the easiest and C is the most challenging.

Lesson Plans

These lesson plans follow the general sequence of a *Discovering French, Nouveau!–Bleu* lesson. Teachers using these plans should become familiar with both the overall structure of a *Discovering French, Nouveau!–Bleu* lesson and with the format of the lesson plans and available ancillaries before translating these plans to a daily sequence.

Block Scheduling Lesson Plans

These plans are structured to help teachers maximize the advantages of block scheduling, while minimizing the challenges of longer periods.

Family Letter and Family Involvement

This section offers strategies and activities to increase family support for students' study of French language and culture.

Absent Student Copymasters

The Absent Student Copymasters enable students who miss part of a **Leçon** to go over the material on their own. The Absent Student Copymasters also offer strategies and techniques to help students understand new or challenging information. If possible, make a copy of the CD, video, or DVD available, either as a loan to an absent student or for use in the school library or language lab.

Video Activities and Videoscript

The Video Activities that accompany the Video or DVD for each module focus students' attention on each video section and reinforce the material presented in the module. A transcript of the Videoscript is included for each **Leçon**.

Audioscripts

This section provides scripts for the Audio Program and includes vocabulary presentations, dialogues, readings and reading summaries, audio for Workbook and Student Text activities, and audio for Lesson Quizzes.

Communipak

The Communication section contains five types of oral communication activities introduced sequentially by level of challenge or difficulty. Designed to encourage students to use French for communication in conversational exchanges, they include *Interviews*, *Tu as la parole*, *Conversations*, *Échanges*, and *Tête à tête* activities.

Assessment

Lesson Quizzes

The Lesson Quizzes provide short accuracy-based vocabulary and structure assessments. They measure how well students have mastered the new conversational phrases, structures, and vocabulary in the lesson. Also designed to encourage students to review material in a given lesson before continuing further in the unit, the quizzes provide an opportunity for focused cyclical re-entry and review.

Unit Tests

The Unit Tests are intended to be administered upon completion of each unit. They may be given in the language laboratory or in the classroom. The total possible score for each test is 100 points. Scoring suggestions for each section appear on the test sheets. The Answer Key for the Unit Tests appears at the end of the Unit Resource Book.

There is one Unit Test for each of the eight units in *Discovering French, Nouveau!–Bleu*. Each test is available in two versions: Form A and Form B. A complete Audioscript is given for the listening portion of the tests; the recordings of these sections appear on CDs 13–16.

Speaking Performance Test

These tests enable teachers to evaluate students' comprehension, ability to respond in French, and overall fluency. Designed to be administered to students individually, each test consists of two sections, *Conversations* and *Tu as la parole*.

Reading Comprehension Performance Test

These tests allow for evaluation of students' ability to understand material written in French. The Reading Comprehension Performance Test is designed for group administration. Each test contains several reading selections, in a variety of styles. Each selection is accompanied by one to four related multiple-choice questions in English.

Listening Comprehension Performance Test

The Listening Comprehension Test is designed for group administration. Each test contains ten short listening items, each accompanied by a multiple-choice question. The test is divided into two parts, *Conversations* and *Questions et réponses*. The listening selections are recorded on CD, and the full script is also provided so that the teacher can administer the test either by playing the CD or by reading the selections aloud.

Writing Performance Test

The Writing Performance Test gives students the opportunity to demonstrate how well they can use the material in the unit for self-expression. The emphasis is not on the production of specific grammar forms, but rather on the communication of meaning. Each test contains several guided writing activities, which vary in format from unit to unit.

Multiple Choice Test Items

These are the print version of the multiple choice questions from the Test Generator. They are contextualized and focus on vocabulary, grammar, reading, writing, and cultural knowledge.

Answer Key

The Answer Key includes answers that correspond to the following material:
- Video Activities
- Lesson Quizzes
- Communipak Activities
- Unit Tests
- Performance Tests
- Multiple Choice Test Items

Nom _____

Classe _____ Date _____

Discovering
FRENCH *Nouveau!*

B L E U

Unité 5
Leçon 13

Workbook TE

Unité 5. En ville

LEÇON 13   Le français pratique: La ville et la maison

LISTENING ACTIVITIES

Section 1. La ville

A. Compréhension orale

▶ Dans ma rue, il y a . . .
  a. ☑ un hôtel
  b. ☑ un magasin
  c. ☐ un café
  d. ☑ un restaurant

1. Dans ma rue, il y a . . .
   a. ☐ une bibliothèque
   b. ☑ un cinéma
   c ☑ un magasin
   d. ☑ un supermarché

2. Dans mon quartier, il y a . . .
   a. ☑ une église
   b. ☑ une école
   c. ☐ un hôpital
   d. ☑ un café

3. Dans ma ville, il y a . . .
   a. ☑ une bibliothèque
   b. ☐ une église
   c. ☑ un théâtre
   d. ☑ un musée

4. Dans ma ville, il y a aussi . . .
   a. ☐ un supermarché
   b. ☑ un hôpital
   c. ☑ un centre commercial
   d. ☑ une piscine

5. Il y a aussi . . .
   a. ☑ un stade
   b. ☑ une plage
   c. ☑ un parc
   d. ☐ un musée

URB
Lp. 1

Discovering French, Nouveau! Bleu

Unité 5, Leçon 13
Workbook

117

Nom _____

Classe _____ Date _____ _____

B. Questions et réponses

▶ —Qu'est-ce que c'est?
—**C'est un cinéma.**

[CINÉMA image]

C'est une piscine. C'est un restaurant. C'est un centre commerci

C'est une bibliothèque. C'est un café. C'est un hôtel. C'est un magasin.

Section 2. Les directions

C. Compréhension orale

Now you will hear several people asking how to get to certain places. Listen carefully to the answers. Select the corresponding completions in your Workbook.

1. Le Café de l'Univers?
   a. ❑ C'est tout droit.
   b. ☑ C'est là-bas à droite.
   c. ❑ C'est là-bas à gauche.

2. Le Grand Hôtel?
   a. ❑ C'est loin.
   b. ☑ Ce n'est pas très loin.
   c. ❑ C'est à côté *(next door)*.

3. Un restaurant?
   a. ❑ Là-bas, vous tournez à gauche.
   b. ☑ Là-bas, vous tournez à droite.
   c. ❑ Là-bas, vous allez tout droit.

4. La cathédrale?
   a. ❑ Vous continuez tout droit.
   b. ❑ Vous tournez à droite et vous continuez tout droit.
   c. ☑ Vous tournez à gauche et vous continuez tout droit.

Nom _____

Classe _____ Date _____

Discovering
FRENCH
Nouveau!

B L E U

Unité 5
Leçon 13

Workbook TE

D. Écoutez et répétez.

 C'est tout droit.

C'est à droite.

C'est à gauche.

 C'est en haut.

C'est en bas.

Section 3. La maison

E. Compréhension orale

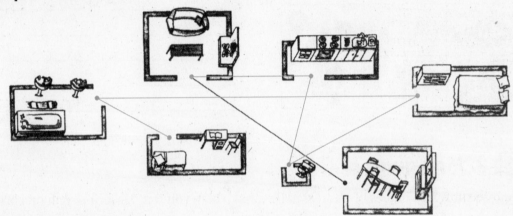

F. Questions et réponses

Modèle: —Où est la cuisine?
—C'est à droite.

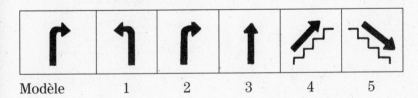

Modèle   1   2   3   4   5

1. C'est à gauche.
2. C'est à droite.
3. C'est tout droit.
4. C'est en haut.
5. C'est en bas.

Section 4. Dictée

G. Écoutez et écrivez.

—Pardon, mademoiselle, où est l'Hôtel _____ des Anglais?

—Il est dans la rue _____ de la République.

—C'est loin _____?

—Non, vous tournez à gauche _____ et vous continuez tout droit _____.

—Merci.

URB
Lp. 3

Discovering French, Nouveau! Bleu

Unité 5, Leçon 13
Workbook

119

Unité 5
Leçon 13

Workbook TE

Nom _____

Classe _____ Date _____

Discovering
FRENCH
Nouveau!

B L E U

WRITING ACTIVITIES

A/B **1. Bienvenue à Bellerive-du-Lac** *(Welcome to Bellerive-du-Lac)*

Imagine that you are spending your vacation in the small French town of Bellerive-du-Lac. The various facilities that the town has to offer are represented on an information panel. List as many of these facilities as you can.

BIENVENUE À
BELLERIVE-DU-LAC
INFORMATION

À Bellerive, il y a . . .

(1) un hôtel _____

(2) un café _____

(3) un restaurant _____

(4) une piscine _____

(5) un stade _____

(6) un parc _____

(7) un cinéma _____

(8) une bibliothèque _____

(9) une église _____

A/B **2. Mon quartier** (sample answers)

Name three different places of interest in the area where you live. Describe each one briefly.

▶ Dans mon quartier, il y a un restaurant français. Il s'appelle Chez Tante Louise.
C'est un assez bon restaurant.

1. Dans mon quartier, il y a un supermarché. Il s'appelle Broadway Supermarket.
C'est un assez grand supermarché.

2. Dans ma ville, il y a un parc. Il s'appelle Heckscher Park.
C'est un très grand parc.

3. Il y a aussi un musée. Il s'appelle The Sackler Museum.
C'est un musée intéressant.

Discovering
FRENCH
Nouveau!
B L E U

Unité 5
Leçon 13
Workbook TE

Classe _____ Date _____

C/D 3. Où est-ce?

Imagine that you are living in a French town. Someone is asking you for directions. Help the person out, according to the suggestions.

▶ —Pardon, où est l'hôtel Beau-Rivage?

—C'est _tout droit_.

1. —S'il vous plaît, où est l'hôpital Velpeau?

—C'est _à droite_.

2. —Excusez-moi, où est la bibliothèque municipale?

—C'est _à gauche_.

3. —Pardon, où sont les toilettes?

—C'est _en haut_.

4. — S'il vous plaît, où est le garage?

—C'est _en bas_.

D 4. Ma maison (sample answers)

Draw a floor plan of your house or apartment. Label each room. (If you prefer, you can draw the floor plan of your dream house.)

chambre de mes parents	salle de bains	cuisine	salle à manger
chambre de ma soeur	salle de bains	ma chambre	le salon

Nom _____

Classe _____ Date _____

Discovering
FRENCH
Nouveau!

BLEU

Unité 5
Leçon 13

Activités pour tous TE

Unité 5. En ville

LEÇON 13 Le français pratique: La ville et la maison

A

Activité 1 Une invitation

A French-speaking exchange student is asking you about where you live. Making your selections from the box, complete the following dialogue. Use each selection once.

quartier	dans	loin	près	ville

—Est-ce que tu habites en <u>ville</u> ?

—Oui. J'habite <u>dans</u> l'avenue Roosevelt.

—Et ton <u>quartier</u>, il est sympathique?

—Oui, très. Je veux inviter les copains à la maison.

—C'est <u>loin</u> ?

—Oh non, c'est <u>près</u> ! C'est pratique!

Activité 2 Charades

Making your selections from the box, guess the places that fit the descriptions.

un parc	une bibliothèque	une piscine	un musée	un stade

1. Là, il y a des livres.   C'est <u>une bibliothèque</u>.
2. Là, je peux nager.   C'est <u>une piscine</u>.
3. Là, je fais des promenades.   C'est <u>un parc</u>.
4. Là, nous faisons un match.   C'est <u>un stade</u>.
5. C'est artistique.   C'est <u>un musée</u>.

Activité 3 La maison

Look at the floor plan on the next page and decide if these statements are true or false.

1. Les chambres sont en bas.   Vrai   (Faux)
2. Il y a quatre lits.   (Vrai)   Faux
3. Il y a un salon.   (Vrai)   Faux
4. Il y a trois salles de bains.   Vrai   (Faux)
5. Il n'y a pas de garage.   (Vrai)   Faux

Nom _____

Classe _____ Date _____

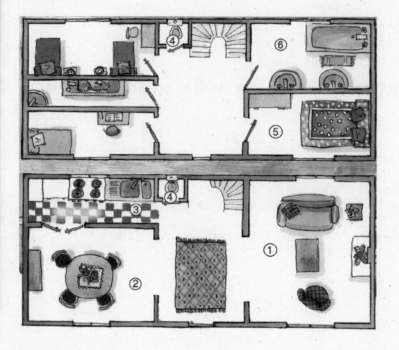

(en haut)

(en bas)

B

Activité 1   La maison

You are visiting a new house, shown above, with your parents and a real estate agent. As you go from room to room, following the numbers, fill in the blanks.

① Nous visitons _le salon_ .

② Nous sommes dans _la salle à manger_ .

③ Je visite _la cuisine_ .

④ Ce sont _les toilettes_ .

⑤ _La chambre_ est bien grande.

⑥ Je suis dans _la salle be bains_ .

Activité 2   Vrai ou faux?

If the following statements are generally true, circle **Vrai.** If not, circle **Faux.**

1. Dans un centre commercial, il y a des magasins.   (Vrai)   Faux

2. Une piscine, c'est pour étudier.   Vrai   (Faux)

3. Les jardins sont en haut.   Vrai   (Faux)

4. Il y a beaucoup de livres dans une bibliothèque.   (Vrai)   Faux

Activité 3   Questions

Match the question with the most logical response.

_e_   1. Où est-ce qu'il y a un hôtel?

_a_   2. Est-ce que c'est près?

_b_   3. Tournez à droite et voilà!

_d_   4. Où habites-tu?

_c_   5. Comment est ta ville?

a. Non, c'est assez loin.

b. Merci beaucoup, monsieur.

c. Elle est très intéressante.

d. J'habite à Boston.

e. Dans la rue à gauche.

Nom _____

Classe _____ Date _____

Discovering
FRENCH *Nouveau!*

BLEU

Unité 5
Leçon 13
Activités pour tous TE

C

Activité 1 Questions (Sample answers)

You are telling a pen pal in France about your town. Fill in the blanks with the information you want to convey.

1. J'habite _à Ridgewood_ .

2. Dans ma ville, il y a _des magasins_ , _des restaurants_ et _un cinéma_ .

3. Mais il n'y a pas _de musées_ ou _d'hôtel_ .

Activité 2 Le plan de la ville

Answer the following questions based on the illustration.

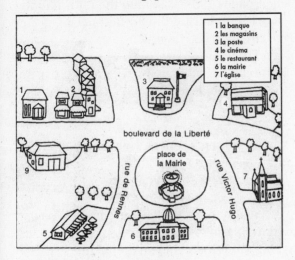

1 la banque
2 les magasins
3 la poste
4 le cinéma
5 le restaurant
6 la mairie
7 l'église

boulevard de la Liberté

place de la Mairie

rue de Rennes

rue Victor Hugo

1. Dans quelle rue est le restaurant? _Il est dans la rue de Rennes_ .

2. Tu es au restaurant. Est-ce que la mairie est loin? _Non, elle est près_ .

3. Tu es à la mairie. Où est l'église? _Elle est à droite_

4. Tu es dans la place de la Mairie. Où est la poste? _Elle est devant moi / Elle est tout droit_

Activité 3 Ma maison (sample answers)

Alysée, a new exchange student from France, is asking you about your home. Answer her questions.

—Est-ce que tu habites dans une maison ou un immeuble?

— _J'habite dans un immeuble_ .

—Est-ce qu'il y a un jardin?

— _Oui, il y a un petit jardin_ .

—Il y a combien de chambres chez toi?

— _Il y a trois chambres_ .

—Comment est ta chambre?

— _Elle est grande et bleue, avec une fenêtre_ .

LEÇON 13 Le français pratique: La ville et la maison, page 194

Objectives

Communicative Functions and Topics
To identify and describe city places, streets, buildings, and neighborhoods
To ask for and give directions
To give your address
To describe the inside and outside of your home

Linguistic Goals To use impersonal *il y a* and *c'est*

Cultural Goals To learn about two French cities: Paris and Tours

Motivation and Focus

❑ Have students look at the photo in the *Unit Opener*, pages 192–193. Share the information in the PHOTO CULTURE NOTE, page 193 of the TE. Discuss similarities and differences between Paris and their city or town. Read *Thème et Objectifs*, page 192.

❑ Do SETTING THE SCENE, page 194 of the TE. Then read together *Accent sur . . .* , page 194, and the descriptions of places in the city of Tours on page 195. Share the CULTURAL NOTE in the TE margin.

Presentation and Explanation

❑ *Vocabulary A:* Present page 196, modeling and having students repeat. Help students describe their city or town and give their own addresses in French.

❑ *Note culturelle:* Read *Le nom des rues*, page 196. Discuss streets in your city or town that are named after famous people.

❑ *Vocabulary B:* Use **Overhead Transparencies** 30a and b to introduce place names, page 197. Have students identify places that are located in their city or town.

❑ *Vocabulary C:* Introduce page 199, asking and giving directions. As you model the sentences, help clarify meaning with gestures and intonation.

❑ *Vocabulary D:* To present rooms of the house, page 200, use **Overhead Transparency** 31. Share the LANGUAGE and CULTURAL NOTES on page 200 of the TE. Model and have students repeat the expressions; guide them to describe their own homes.

Guided Practice and Checking Understanding

❑ Use **Overhead Transparencies** 30a and b, 31, and 32, with the activities on pages A88–A94, to practice talking about cities and houses and giving directions.

❑ Check students' listening skills with **Audio CD** 9, Tracks 1–7 or the **Audioscript,** and **Workbook** Listening Activities A–G on pages 117–119.

❑ Have students do **Video Activities** pages 21–25 as they watch the **Video** or listen to the **Videoscript** for the lesson.

❑ Do the COMPREHENSION activities on places, pages 196–197 of the TE, and on rooms of the house, pages 200–201 of the TE.

Independent Practice

❑ Do the practice activities on pages 196–201. Do 1, 3, and 6–8 for homework. Model Activities 2, 4, and 5 before having students do them as PAIR PRACTICE.

❑ Use **Communipak** *Conversations* 1–2, pages 145–146, and *Tête à tête* 1, pages 153–154. Students can prepare floor plans with **Video Activities** page 26.

❑ Have students do the activities in **Activités pour tous,** pages 71–73.

Discovering
FRENCH *Nouveau!*

B L E U

Unité 5
Leçon 13

Lesson Plans

Monitoring and Adjusting

❑ Assign Writing Activities 1–4 in the **Workbook**, pages 120–121.
❑ Monitor use of place names and directions as students do the activities. Refer students to the vocabulary on pages 196–200. Use the TEACHING NOTE on page 198 of the TE with Activity 3.

Assessment

❑ After completing all of the lesson's activities, use Quiz 13 on pages 33–34. Adjust lesson quizzes to meet student's needs by using the **Test Generator**.

Reteaching

❑ Redo any appropriate activities in the **Workbook**.
❑ Assign **Teacher to Teacher**, page 12.
❑ Assign portions of the **Video** to reteach parts of the lesson

Extension and Enrichment

❑ Use SUPPLEMENTARY VOCABULARY on pages 196–197, 200 of the TE, and the CHALLENGE ACTIVITIES on page 203 of the TE, to challenge more advanced students.
❑ Have students make a map of their city as described at the bottom of page 199 of the TE.

Summary and Closure

❑ Help summarize the vocabulary and expressions of the lesson. Then ask students to demonstrate by using **Overhead Transparency** S13 and the first activity on page A26 or Transparency 32 and the activities on A94, or by describing their house.
❑ Do PORTFOLIO ASSESSMENT on page 202 of the TE.

End-of-Lesson Activities

❑ *À votre tour!:* Students can prepare and practice Activities 1–3, pages 202 and 203. Follow the suggestions on page 202 of the TE for GROUP PRACTICE in trios. Assign Activity 5 for written homework.

LEÇON 13 Le français pratique:
La ville et la maison, page 194

Block Scheduling (3 days to complete)

Objectives

Communicative Functions and Topics	To identify and describe city places, streets, buildings, and neighborhoods To ask for and give directions To give your address To describe the inside and outside of your home
Linguistic Goals	To use impersonal *il y a* and *c'est*
Cultural Goals	To learn about two French cities: Paris and Tours

Day 1

Motivation and Focus

❑ Have students look at the photo in the *Unit Opener*, pages 192–193. Share the information in the PHOTO CULTURE NOTES, page 193 of the TE. Discuss similarities and differences between Paris and their city or town. Read *Thème et Objectifs*, page 192.

❑ Do SETTING THE SCENE, page 194 of the TE. Then read together *Accent sur . . .*, page 194, and the descriptions of places in the city of Tours on page 195. Share the CULTURAL NOTE in the TE margin.

Presentation and Explanation

❑ *Vocabulary A:* Present page 196, modeling and having students repeat. Help students describe their city or town and give their own addresses in French.

❑ *Note culturelle:* Read *Le nom des rues*, page 196. Discuss streets in your city or town that are named after famous people.

❑ *Vocabulary B:* Use **Overhead Transparencies** 30a and b to introduce place names, page 197. Have students identify places that are located in their city or town.

❑ *Vocabulary C:* Introduce page 199, asking and giving directions. As you model the sentences, help clarify meaning with gestures and intonation.

❑ *Vocabulary D:* To present rooms of the house, page 200, use **Overhead Transparency** 31. Share the LANGUAGE and CULTURAL NOTES on page 200 of the TE. Model and have students repeat the expressions; guide them to describe their own homes.

Guided Practice and Checking Understanding

❑ Use **Overhead Transparencies** 30a and b, 31, and 32, with the activities on pages A88 and A74–A94, to practice talking about cities and houses and giving directions.

❑ Check students' listening skills with **Audio CD** 9, Tracks 1–7 or the **Audioscript**, and **Workbook** Listening Activities A–G on pages 117–119.

Discovering
FRENCH
Nouveau!

BLEU

Unité 5
Leçon 13

Block Scheduling
Lesson Plans

Day 2

Motivation and Focus

❏ Have students do **Video Activities** pages 21–25 as they watch the **Video** or listen to the **Videoscript** for the lesson.

Teaching with Discovering French

❏ Do the COMPREHENSION activities on places, pages 196–197 of the TE, and on rooms of the house, pages 200–201 of the TE.

Independent Practice

❏ Do the practice activities on pages 196–201. Do 1, 3, and 6–8 for homework. Model Activities 2, 4, and 5 before having students do them as PAIR PRACTICE.
❏ Use **Communipak** *Conversations* 1–2, pages 145–146, and *Tête à tête* 1, pages 153–154. Students can prepare floor plans with **Video Activities** page 26.
❏ Have students do the activities in **Activités pour tous,** pages 71–73.

Monitoring and Adjusting

❏ Assign Writing Activities 1–4 in the **Workbook**, pages 120–121.
❏ Monitor use of place names and directions as students do the activities. Refer students to the vocabulary on pages 196–200. Use the TEACHING NOTE on page 198 of the TE with activity 3.

Day 3

End-of-Lesson Activities

❏ *À votre tour!:* Students can prepare Activities 1–3, pages 202 and 203. Follow the suggestions on page 202 of the TE for GROUP PRACTICE in trios. Assign Activity 5 for written homework.

Reteaching (as needed)

❏ Redo activities in the **Workbook** and assign **Teacher to Teacher**, page 12.
❏ Use portions of the **Video** to reteach parts of the lesson.

Extension and Enrichment (as desired)

❏ Use SUPPLEMENTARY VOCABULARY on pages 196–197, 200 of the TE, and the CHALLENGE ACTIVITIES on page 203 of the TE, to challenge more advanced students.
❏ Have students make a map of their city as described at the bottom on page 199 of the TE.
❏ Use **Block Scheduling Copymasters,** pages 97–104.
❏ For expansion activities, direct students to www.classzone.com.

Summary and Closure

❏ Use **Overhead Transparency** S13 and the first activity on page A26 or Transparency 32 and the activities on A94. Have students describe their houses.
❏ Do PORTFOLIO ASSESSMENT on page 202 of the TE.

Assessment

❏ After completing all of the lesson's activities, use Quiz 13 on pages 33–34. Adjust lesson quizzes to meet students' needs by using the **Test Generator**.

BLEU

Date:

Dear Family,

Right now, we are studying Unit 5 of the *Discovering French, Nouveau!–Bleu* program. This unit focuses on authentic culture and real-life communication skills as students use French to find their way around a French city.

In this unit, students are learning to describe their city and neighborhood, to ask and give directions, to talk about the places they go and the things they are going to do, to describe their house or apartment, and to talk about their family. They are also learning about grammar—learning to conjugate the irregular verbs **aller** *(to go)* and **venir** *(to come)*, and learning to form contractions and to show possession using possessive pronouns.

While completing the activities in this unit, students employ critical thinking skills as they compare the French language and the culture of France with their own community.

Please feel free to call me with any questions or concerns you might have as your student practices reading, writing, listening, and speaking in French.

Sincerely,

Nom

Classe _____ Date _____

Discovering
FRENCH
Nouveau!

BLEU

Unité 5
Leçon 13

Absent Student Copymasters

LEÇON 13 Le français pratique: La ville et la maison, pages 192–195

Materials Checklist

- **Student Text**
- **Video** 3 or **DVD** 2; Counter 0:10–7:02

Steps to Follow

- Unit Opener: Look at the photographs on pages 192–194. Is the building in the background a public building or a private building? How can you tell? What do you notice about the building's surroundings? Is this a playground or a park? How can you tell?
- Read *Accent sur . . . les villes françaises* (p. 194).
- Watch **Video** 3 or **DVD** 2 Counter 0:10–7:02.
- Read the chart *The largest French cities* (p. 194). As you read the chart, find each city mentioned in it on the map.
- Read the information about Tours (p. 195).
- Look at the photos on p. 195 and read the captions.
- Write the captions on a separate sheet of paper. Underline all the words you recognize. Circle the new words and check their meanings.

If You Don't Understand . . .

- Watch the **Video** or **DVD** in a quiet room. Try to stay focused. If you get lost, stop the **Video** or **DVD**. Replay it and find your place in the text.
- Write down questions on a sheet of paper so that you can ask your partner or your teacher later.

Self-Check

Answer the following questions on a separate sheet of paper.

1. À Tours, où est l'hôtel de ville?
2. Est-ce que la place Plumereau est un endroit très animé?
3. Est-ce que Tours a un château historique?
4. Où habitent les Français qui n'habitent pas dans le centre-ville?

Answers

1. À Tours, l'hôtel de ville est au centre. 2. Oui, la place Plumereau est un endroit très animé. 3. Oui, Tours a un château historique. 4. Les Français qui n'habitent pas dans le centre ville habitent dans une maison individuelle.

Nom _____

Classe _____ Date _____

Discovering
FRENCH
Nouveau!

BLEU

A. Vocabulaire: Où habites-tu? page 196

Materials Checklist

- **Student Text**
- **Workbook**

Steps to Follow

- Study Vocabulaire: *Où habites-tu?* (p. 196).
- On a separate sheet of paper, write the new expressions.
- Read the *Note culturelle* (p. 196).
- Do Activity 1 in the text (p. 196). Write the answers in complete sentences on a separate sheet of paper.
- Do Activity 2 in the text (p. 196). Write the interview questions on a separate sheet of paper. Look at the new vocabulary as necessary to refresh your memory.
- Do **Writing Activities** A 1 in the **Workbook** (p. 120).

If You Don't Understand . . .

- Watch the **Video** or **DVD** in a quiet place. Try to stay focused. If you get lost, stop the **Video** or **DVD**. Replay it and find your place.
- Reread the activity directions. Put the directions in your own words.
- Say aloud everything that you write. Be sure you understand what you are saying.
- Write down questions so that you can ask your partner or your teacher later.

Self-Check

Answer the following questions on a separate sheet of paper. Write complete sentences.

1. Est-ce que tu habites dans une grande ville?
2. Est-ce que tu habites dans un petit village?
3. Est-ce que tu habites dans un joli quartier?
4. Est-ce que tu habites dans une rue intéressante?
5. Est-ce que Victor Hugo est un grand poète?
6. Est-ce que La Fayette est célèbre?

Answers

1. Oui, j'habite dans une grande ville. / Non, je n'habite pas dans une grande ville. 2. Oui, j'habite dans un petit village. / Non, je n'habite pas dans un petit village. 3. Oui, j'habite dans un joli quartier. / Non, je n'habite pas dans un joli quartier. 4. Oui, j'habite dans une rue intéressante. / Non, je n'habite pas dans une rue intéressante. 5. Oui, Victor Hugo est un grand poète. 6. Oui, La Fayette est célèbre.

Nom _____

Classe _____ Date _____

Discovering
FRENCH
Nouveau!

B L E U

B. Vocabulaire: Ma ville, pages 197–198

Materials Checklist

- **Student Text**
- **Audio CD** 9, Tracks 1–2
- **Video** 3 or **DVD** 2; Counter 4:07–5:10
- **Workbook**

Steps to Follow

- Study *Vocabulaire: Ma ville* (p. 197).
- Use the new vocabulary to write complete sentences on a separate sheet of paper. Underline the new expressions, for example, **Dans ma rue**, il y a un hôtel. Say each sentence aloud.
- Watch **Video** 3 or **DVD** 2; Counter 4:07–5:10.
- Do Activities 3 and 4 in the text (p. 198). Write the answers in complete sentences on a separate sheet of paper. Say each sentence aloud.
- Do **Writing Activities** A/B 2 in the **Workbook** (p. 120).
- Do **Listening Activities** A–B in the **Workbook** (pp. 117–118). Use **Audio CD** 9, Tracks 1–2.

If You Don't Understand . . .

- Watch the **Video** or **DVD** in a quiet place. Try to stay focused. If you get lost, stop the **Video** or **DVD**. Replay it and find your place.
- Listen to the **CD** in a quiet place. Try to stay focused. If you get lost, stop the **CD**. Replay it and find your place.
- Reread the activity directions. Put the directions in your own words.
- Say aloud everything that you write. Be sure you understand what you are saying.
- Write down questions so that you can ask your partner or your teacher later.

Self-Check

Answer the following questions on a separate sheet of paper. Write complete sentences.

1. Est-ce qu'il y a un restaurant dans le quartier? (oui)
2. Est-ce qu'il y a un cinéma dans la rue? (oui)
3. Est-ce qu'il y a une bibliothèque dans le quartier? (non)
4. Est-ce qu'il y a un parc dans la ville? (oui)
5. Est-ce qu'il y a un stade dans la ville? (non)
6. Est-ce qu'il y a une piscine dans le quartier? (non)

Answers

1. Oui, il y a un restaurant dans le quartier. 2. Oui, il y a un cinéma dans la rue. 3. Non, il n'y a pas de bibliothèque dans le quartier. 4. Oui, il y a un parc dans la ville. 5. Non, il n'y a pas de stade dans la ville. 6. Non, il n'y a pas de piscine dans le quartier.

Nom _____

Classe _____ Date _____

Unité 5
Leçon 13

Absent Student Copymasters

Discovering
FRENCH
Nouveau!

B L E U

C. Vocabulaire: Pour demander un renseignement; page 199
D. Vocabulaire: Ma maison, pages 200–201

Materials Checklist

- **Student Text**
- **Audio CD** 3, Tracks 1–3; **CD** 9, Tracks 3–7
- **Video** 3 or **DVD** 2; Counter 5:11–7:02
- **Workbook**

Steps to Follow

- Study *Vocabulaire: Pour demander un renseignement* (p. 199). Write the new expressions on a separate sheet of paper. Read them aloud.
- Watch **Video** 3 or **DVD** 2; Counter 5:11–7:02.
- Do Activity 5 in the text (p. 199). For each dialogue, write the questions and answers for both speakers. Read both parts aloud.
- Study *Vocabulaire: Ma maison* (p. 200). Write the expressions on a separate sheet of paper. Read them aloud.
- Do Activities 6, 7, and 8 in the text (p. 200). Write the answers in complete sentences.
- Do **Writing Activities** C/D 3 and D 4 in the **Workbook** (p. 121).
- Do **Listening Activities** C–G in the **Workbook** (pp. 118–119). Use **Audio CD** 9, Tracks 3–7.
- Do Activities 1–5 of *À votre tour!* in the text (pp. 202–203). Use **Audio CD** 3, Tracks 1–3 with Activities 1, 3 and 4.

If You Don't Understand . . .

- Watch the **Video** or **DVD** in a quiet place. Try to stay focused. If you get lost, stop the **Video** or **DVD**. Replay it and find your place.
- Listen to the **CDs** in a quiet place. Try to stay focused. If you get lost, stop the **CDs** and find your place.
- Reread the activity directions. Put the directions in your own words.
- Say aloud everything that you write. Be sure you understand what you are saying.
- Write down questions so that you can ask your partner or your teacher later.

Self-Check

Answer the following questions on a separate sheet of paper. Write complete sentences.

1. Où est ta chambre? (en haut)
2. Où est la cuisine? (en bas)
3. Où sont les toilettes? (en haut)
4. Où est le restaurant? (à gauche)
5. Où est l'hôtel? (dans la rue St-Jean)
6. Est-ce que c'est loin? (près)

Answers

1. Ma chambre est en haut. 2. La cuisine est en bas. 3. Les toilettes sont en haut. 4. Le restaurant est à gauche. 5. L'hôtel est dans la rue St-Jean. 6. Non c'est près.

Nom _____

Classe _____ Date _____

Discovering
FRENCH
Nouveau!

B L E U

LEÇON 13 La ville et la maison

Mon quartier

Interview a family member about your neighborhood.

- First, explain your assignment.
- Model the pronunciation of the words below each picture. Be sure to point to the picture as you model each answer.
- Then, ask the question: **Qu'est-ce qu'il y a dans le quartier?**
- After you have received an answer, complete the sentences at the bottom of the page.

une école

un parc

une église

une bibliothèque

un supermarché

un restaurant

Dans mon quartier, il y a _____.

Dans mon quartier, il n'y a pas de _____.

Nom _____

Classe _____ Date _____

Où aimes-tu manger?

Interview a family member about where he or she prefers to eat.

- First, explain your assignment.
- Model the pronunciation of the words below the pictures of the rooms. Point to the picture as you model each answer.
- Ask the question: **Où est-ce que tu préfères manger?**
- When you have an answer, complete the sentence at the bottom of the page.

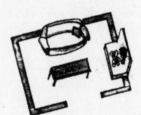

le salon

la salle à manger

la cuisine

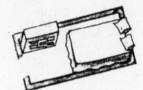

la chambre

_____ préfère manger dans _____.

Discovering
FRENCH
Nouveau!

BLEU

Unité 5
Leçon 13
Video Activities

MODULE 13 Le français pratique: La ville et la maison

Video 3, DVD 2

🌐 **13.1 Activité 1.** Challenge activity: *Les villes de France*   Counter 0:10–1:09

After looking at the map on the video, complete this map of France by writing the name of each city listed in the box in the appropriate blank.

Paris	Marseille	Lyon	Lille	Bordeaux
Toulouse	Nantes	Toulon	Grenoble	Strasbourg

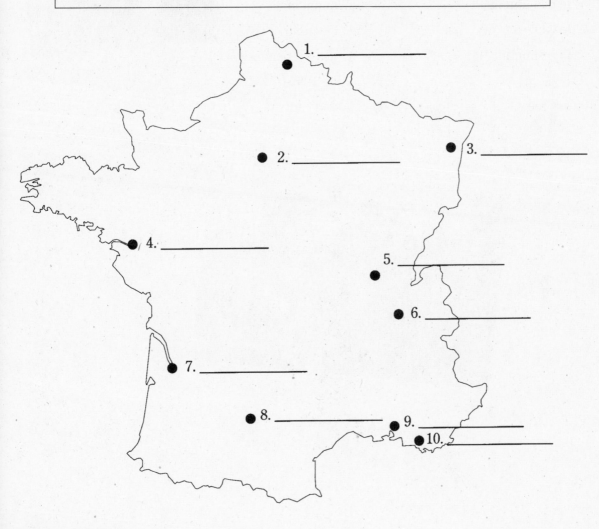

Discovering French, Nouveau! Bleu

Nom _____

Classe _____ Date _____

Discovering
FRENCH
Nouveau!

B L E U

13.2 Activité 2. La ville de Tours

Counter 1:10–4:06

As Olivier takes you around Tours in the video, complete the name of each place by drawing a line from each item on the left to the appropriate completion on the right. (*Note:* The items in the left-hand column appear in the order in which you see them on the video.)

1. le Palais . . .   a. américain
2. le Café . . .   b. Buré
3. les Nouvelles . . .   c. Descartes
4. la cathédrale . . .   d. Galeries
5. la bibliothèque . . .   e. de Justice
6. le monument . . .   f. municipale
7. le lycée . . .   g. Olympia
8. le restaurant . . .   h. des Prébendes
9. le jardin . . .   i. de Tours
10. le Cinéma . . .   j. de l'Univers

Nom _____

Classe _____ Date _____

13.3 Activité 3. Qu'est-ce que c'est?

Counter 4:07–5:10

After watching the video segment, look at the pictures below. Then fill in the blank sign in each illustration with the appropriate place name from the box.

centre commercial	piscine	bibliothèque	hôtel
café	cinéma	restaurant	magasin

1.

2.

3.

4.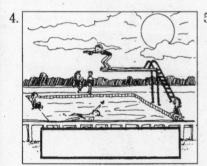

5.

6.

7.

8.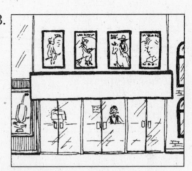

13.4 Activité 4. Pardon. Excusez-moi!

Counter 5:11–6:02

Listen and watch as Olivier gives people directions to four places in Tours. For each destination, mark an **X** under each piece of information Olivier gives as you hear it. (*Note:* There may be more than one answer for some items.)

	à gauche	tout droit	à droite	pas loin/ près	loin
1. le Café de l'Univers					
2. le Grand Hôtel					
3. un restaurant					
4. la cathédrale					

Discovering
FRENCH *Nouveau!*

B L E U

Unité 5
Leçon 13

Video Activities

🌐 **13.5 Activité 5.** La maison d'Olivier

As Olivier takes you through his house, number the rooms in the order in which he shows them to you. Start with 1 and end with 7.

a. _____ le salon

b. _____ ma chambre

c. _____ la cuisine

d. _____ des toilettes

e. _____ la salle à manger

f. _____ la salle de bains

g. _____ la chambre de mes parents

 **Activité 6.** Votre maison

In the space below, draw a floor plan of your
house or apartment and label the rooms. Then
share floor plans with your partner by going
through your plan and naming the rooms.

▶**Voici ma maison. En bas, il y a la
cuisine, une salle de bains et le salon.
En haut, il y a . . .**

MODULE 13   Le français pratique: La ville et la maison

Video 3, DVD 2

13.1 Introduction: Listening— Les villes de France   Counter 0:10–1:09

Where do you live, in a small town or in a large city? France has many villages, lots of medium-size cities and a few large cities.

The largest city in France is Paris, the capital. With a population of almost 10 million, Paris is one of the largest metropolitan areas in the world. According to many people, it is also one of the most beautiful. Let's look at the map of France. The next largest cities in France are:

- *Marseille, a large port city on the Mediterranean*
- *Lyon, which was the capital of France in Roman times, and*
- *Lille, in northern France.*

Other important cities are: Bordeaux, Toulouse, Nantes, Toulon, Grenoble, and Strasbourg.

13.2 Dialogue: La ville de Tours
Counter 1:10–4:06

*Today we will visit Tours, a beautiful city located south of Paris in the Loire Valley. The Tours metropolitan area has about 250,000 residents. It is typically French, with a mix of both old and new. Our guide will be Olivier LeGrand, who lives in Tours. **Bonjour, Olivier!***

OLIVIER: Bonjour, je m'appelle Olivier LeGrand. J'habite à Tours. Ici, nous sommes au centre de la ville. À droite, c'est l'hôtel de ville. À gauche, c'est le Palais de Justice. Ici nous sommes Avenue de Grammont. Voici le Café de l'Univers. C'est un café où je viens souvent avec mes copains.
—Salut.
—Salut, Olivier!
—Ça va?

OLIVIER: Nous sommes maintenant rue Nationale. C'est la rue principale de la ville. Voici les Nouvelles Galeries. C'est un magasin.
Ici nous sommes dans le vieux Tours. C'est un quartier très ancien. Regardez les maisons. Elles ont trois cents ans ou quatre cents ans. Voici la cathédrale de Tours. C'est une cathédrale de style gothique. Et voici le musée. Venez voir. Voici le château de Tours.
Et voici la bibliothèque municipale. Regardez le monument là-bas. C'est un monument américain. Il commémore l'aide américaine pendant la première guerre. Et voici mon école. C'est le lycée Descartes.
Ici c'est la piscine municipale. En été, je viens souvent nager ici. Voici le restaurant Buré. C'est un très bon restaurant . . . mais malheureusement trop cher pour moi.
Ça, c'est le César. C'est le restaurant où je vais avec mes copains.
Voici un parc. C'est le jardin des Prébendes.
Regardez ces fleurs! C'est beau, hein?
Ça, c'est le Cinéma Olympia. Et ça, c'est ma maison. Au revoir!

13.3 Mini-scenes: Speaking— Qu'est-ce que c'est?
Counter 4:07–5:10

Now it's your turn to identify different places. Watch.

—Qu'est-ce que c'est?   [screen card]
—C'est un cinéma.

—Qu'est-ce que c'est?   [screen card]
—C'est une piscine.

—Qu'est-ce que c'est?   [screen card]
—C'est un restaurant.

—Qu'est-ce que c'est?   [screen card]
—C'est un centre commercial.

—Qu'est-ce que c'est?   [screen card]
—C'est une bibliothèque.

—Qu'est-ce que c'est?   [screen card]
—C'est un café.

— Qu'est-ce que c'est?   [screen card]
— C'est un hôtel.

— Qu'est-ce que c'est?   [screen card]
— C'est un magasin.

13.4 Mini-scenes: Listening— Pardon! Excusez-moi!

Counter 5:11–6:02

Now you know many names of places in French. When you visit France, you should be able to ask your way around. Watch.

—Pardon! Où est le Café de l'Univers?
—C'est là-bas à droite.
—Merci.

—Excusez-moi. Où est le Grand Hôtel?
—C'est place de la Gare.
—Est-ce que c'est loin?
—Non, ce n'est pas très loin.
—Merci.

—Est-ce qu'il y a un restaurant près d'ici?
—Oui, il y a un restaurant dans la rue de Bordeaux.
—C'est tout droit?
—Non, vous tournez à droite là-bas.
—Merci.

—Excusez-moi. Où est la cathédrale?
—Vous tournez à gauche et vous continuez tout droit.
—C'est loin?
—Non, ce n'est pas très loin.
—Merci.
—Au revoir.

13.5 Vignette culturelle: La maison d'Olivier

Counter 6:03–7:02

OLIVIER: À nouveau, bonjour! Eh bien voilà où j'habite. C'est ma maison.

Olivier has taken us around Tours, the city where he lives. Now he's going to show us around his house. Let's follow him in.

Voici la salle à manger. Voici le salon. Voici la cuisine. Là, il y a des toilettes. Voici la chambre de mes parents. Voici la salle de bains. Et voici ma chambre. Mais dis donc, Malice. Qu'est-ce que tu fais sur mon lit? Allez, va-t'en!

Discovering
FRENCH
Nouveau!

BLEU

Unité 5
Leçon 13

Audioscripts

LEÇON 13   Le français pratique: La ville et la maison

PE AUDIO

À votre tour!

CD 3, Track 1

1. Écoutez bien!, p. 202

Look at the map of Villeneuve. You will hear where certain people are. If they are somewhere on the left side of the map, mark A. If they are on the right side of the map, mark B.

Listen carefully. Do not worry if you do not understand every word. Pay attention to the place name that is mentioned. You will hear each sentence twice. Let's begin.

1. Isabelle joue au foot au stade municipal. #
2. Catherine passe à la bibliothèque pour prendre des livres. #
3. Mon petit frère joue dans le parc de la ville. #
4. Ma mère travaille à l'hôpital Sainte Anne. #
5. Julie et Thomas voient un film au ciné Rex. #
6. Nous sommes au musée pour l'exposition d'art moderne. #
7. Qu'est-ce que vous faites au supermarché? #
8. Ma soeur travaille dans un magasin de sport. #

CD 3, Track 2

3. Créa-dialogue, p. 203

Listen to some sample *Créa-dialogues.*
Écoutez les conversations.

Modèle: —Pardon, monsieur. Où est-ce qu'il y a un hôtel?
—Il y a un hôtel avenue de Bordeaux.
—Est-ce que c'est loin?
—Non, c'est près.
—Merci beaucoup!

Maintenant, écoutez le dialogue numéro 1.

—Pardon, madame. Où est-ce qu'il y a un café?
—Il y a un café avenue de Bordeaux.
—Est-ce que c'est loin?
—Non, c'est près.
—Merci beaucoup!

CD 3, Track 3

4. Où est-ce?, p. 203

Listen to the conversation with the tourist.
Écoutez la conversation avec le touriste.

Modèle: —Pardon monsieur. Où est l'hôpital Sainte Anne?
—C'est tout droit, mademoiselle.
—Merci bien, monsieur.

Voici une autre conversation:

—Pardon, mademoiselle. Où est le musée La Salle?
—Tournez à gauche, rue Danton monsieur.

BLEU

WORKBOOK AUDIO

Section 1. La ville

CD 9, Track 1

A. Compréhension orale, p. 117

You will hear Nathalie show you around her town. In each sentence, she mentions three places. In your Workbook, you will see four places listed. Place a check mark next to the three places you hear. Then draw a circle around the one that she did not mention.

Modèle: Dans ma rue, il y a un hotel, un magasin et un restaurant.

You should have circled "c": **un café.**

1. Dans ma rue, il y a un cinéma, un magasin et un supermarché. #
2. Dans mon quartier, il y a une église, une école et un café. #
3. Dans ma ville, il y a une bibliothèque, un théâtre et un musée. #
4. Dans ma ville, il y a aussi un hôpital, un centre commercial et une piscine. #
5. Il y a aussi un stade, une plage et un parc. #

Now check your answers. You should have circled 1-a, 2-c, 3-b, 4-a, and 5-d.

CD 9, Track 2

B. Questions et réponses, p. 118

Now it's your turn to identify different places. Look at the pictures in your Workbook and answer the questions. If you are not sure of the answer, listen for the confirmation.

Modèle: Qu'est-ce que c'est?
C'est un cinéma.

1. Qu'est-ce que c'est? # C'est une piscine.
2. Qu'est-ce que c'est? # C'est un restaurant.
3. Qu'est-ce que c'est? # C'est un centre commercial.
4. Qu'est-ce que c'est? # C'est une bibliothèque.
5. Qu'est-ce que c'est? # C'est un café.
6. Qu'est-ce que c'est? # C'est un hôtel.
7. Qu'est-ce que c'est? # C'est un magasin.

Section 2. Les directions

CD 9, Track 3

C. Compréhension orale, p. 118

Now you will hear several people asking how to get to certain places. Listen carefully to the answers. Select the corresponding completions in your Workbook.

1. —Pardon! Où est le café de l'Univers?
   —C'est là-bas à droite.
   —Merci. #

2. —Excusez-moi. Où est le Grand Hôtel?
   —C'est place de la Gare.
   —Est-ce que c'est loin?
   —Non, ce n'est pas très loin.
   —Merci. #

3. —Est-ce qu'il y a un restaurant près d'ici?
   —Oui, il y a un restaurant dans la rue de Bordeaux.
   —C'est tout droit?
   —Non, vous tournez à droite là-bas.
   —Merci. #

4. —Excusez-moi. Où est la cathédrale?
   —Vous tournez à gauche et vous continuez tout droit.
   —C'est loin?
   —Non, ce n'est pas très loin.
   —Merci.
   —Au revoir. #

Now check your answers. You should have marked 1-b, 2-b, 3-b, and 4-c.

CD 9, Track 4

D. Écoutez et répétez., p. 119

Repeat the following directions after the speaker.

C'est tout droit. #

C'est à droite. #

C'est à gauche. #

C'est en haut. #

C'est en bas. #

Section 3. La maison

CD 9, Track 5

E. Compréhension orale, p. 119

Now Christophe, a French teenager, is going to take us through his house. In your Workbook you see seven rooms. As Christophe guides us around, draw a line from room to room in the order in which they are pointed out.

Modèle: CHRISTOPHE: Voilà ma maison. Voici la salle à manger.

The first room is the dining room. Place your pencil at "la salle à manger."

CHRISTOPHE: Voici le salon.

Now draw a line over to the living room: "le salon."

Commençons.

CHRISTOPHE: Voici le salon.
Voici la cuisine. #
Là, il y a des toilettes. #
Voici la chambre de mes parents. #
Voici la salle de bains. #
Et voici ma chambre. #

CD 9, Track 6

F. Questions et réponses, p. 119

Someone will ask you where certain rooms are. Answer that person according to the illustration in your Workbook.

Modèle: Où est la cuisine? # C'est à droite.

Commençons.

1. Où est le salon? #

    C'est à gauche.
2. Où est la salle à manger? #

    C'est à droite.
3. Où sont les toilettes? #

    C'est tout droit.
4. Où est ta chambre? #

    C'est en haut.
5. Où est le garage? #

    C'est en bas.

Section 4. Dictée

CD 9, Track 7

G. Écoutez et écrivez., p. 119

You will hear a short dialogue spoken twice. First listen carefully to what the people are saying. The second time you hear the dialogue, fill in the missing words.

Écoutez.

—Pardon, mademoiselle, où est l'Hôtel des Anglais?
—Il est dans la rue de la République.
—C'est loin?
—Non, vous tournez à gauche et vous continuez tout droit.
—Merci.

Listen again and fill in the missing words.

LESSON 13 QUIZ

Part I: Listening

CD 15, Track 1

A. Questions et réponses

You will hear your French friend Charlotte ask you eight questions. Select the MOST LOGICAL response and circle the corresponding letter (a, b, or c). You will hear each question twice.

Let's begin.

1. *Imagine you live in Tours. Charlotte is visiting you from Quebec. She asks:*
   Où est-ce que tu habites?

2. *Charlotte is curious about your neighborhood. She asks:*
   Il y a un supermarché dans ton quartier?

3. *Charlotte does not know her way around. She asks:*
   Où est la rue Nationale?

4. *You are going to invite Charlotte to your house. She asks:*
   Comment est ta chambre?

5. *Charlotte is at your house. It is close to suppertime. She asks:*
   Ton père est à la cuisine?

6. *Charlotte is staying for dinner and it is almost time to eat. She asks:*
   S'il te plaît, où sont les toilettes?

7. *It is Saturday afternoon. You and Charlotte are at a café waiting for Véronique. She asks:*
   Qu'est-ce que Véronique fait à la bibliothèque?

8. *You have talked to Charlotte about your friend Valérie. She asks:*
   Ta copine Valérie est à la piscine?

Nom _____

Classe _____ Date _____

Discovering
FRENCH
Nouveau!

BLEU

Unité 5
Leçon 13

Lesson Quiz

QUIZ 13

PART I: LISTENING

A. Questions et réponses (40 points)

You will hear your French friend Charlotte ask you eight questions. Select the MOST LOGICAL response and circle the corresponding letter (a, b, or c). You will hear each question twice.

1. Imagine you live in Tours. Charlotte is visiting you from Quebec.
   You reply:
   a. Dans le jardin.
   b. 65, rue Émile Zola.
   c. Oui, c'est un joli quartier.

2. Charlotte is curious about your neighborhood.
   You reply:
   a. À gauche.
   b. Non, je n'habite pas ici.
   c. Non, mais il y a un grand centre commercial.

3. Charlotte does not know her way around.
   You reply:
   a. C'est tout droit.
   b. Dans la rue Carnot.
   c. Oui, il y a un magasin là-bas.

4. You are going to invite Charlotte to your house.
   You reply:
   a. Ça va bien, merci!
   b. Petite, mais confortable.
   c. Elle n'est pas méchante.

5. Charlotte is at your house. It is close to suppertime.
   You reply:
   a. Oui, il regarde la télé.
   b. Oui, il prépare le dîner.
   c. Non, il préfère les pizzas.

6. Charlotte is staying for dinner and it is almost time to eat.
   You reply:
   a. En haut, à gauche.
   b. Derrière le garage.
   c. Dans la salle à manger.

7. It is Saturday afternoon. You and Charlotte are at a café waiting for Véronique.
   You reply:
   a. Elle chante.
   b. Elle étudie.
   c. Elle téléphone à un copain.

8. You have talked to Charlotte about your friend Valérie.
   You reply:
   a. Oui, elle aime beaucoup nager.
   b. Oui, elle joue aux jeux vidéo.
   c. Non, elle n'habite pas là.

PART II: WRITING

B. Le bon endroit (32 points)

Write the name of the places where people go to do the things indicated in parentheses. Be sure to use **le, la,** or **l'** before each name.

1. (to see a movie)   _____

2. (to see a play)   _____

3. (to buy food)   _____

4. (to play soccer)   _____

Nom _____

Classe _____ Date _____

Discovering
FRENCH
Nouveau!

B L E U

5. (to buy a jacket)   _____

6. (to borrow a book)   _____

7. (to visit a sick friend)   _____

8. (to see an art exhibit)   _____

C. En ville (12 points)

Monsieur Dupont is not from your town. Tell him how to get
to where he is going by completing the following dialogues
according to the illustrations.

1. —Pardon, où est l'avenue Victor Hugo?

   —_____

2. —Excusez-moi. Où est le boulevard du Maine?

   —_____

3. —Pardon, où est la rue Pascal?

   —_____

D. Expression personnelle (16 points)

Answer the following questions in French. Use complete sentences.

• Do you live in a house or in an apartment building?

  _____

• How many bedrooms and bathrooms are there?

  _____

Nom _____

Classe _____ Date _____

Discovering
FRENCH
Nouveau!

BLEU

Unité 5
Leçon 14

Workbook TE

LEÇON 14 Week-end à Paris

LISTENING ACTIVITIES

Section 1. Je vais à . . .

A. Écoutez et répétez.

1. Je vais en classe.
2. Tu vas au café.
3. Il va au cinéma.
4. Nous allons à une boum.
5. Vous allez à Paris.
6. Ils vont en France.

Section 2. Où vont-ils?

B. Compréhension orale

a. _8_ au stade
b. _3_ au café
c. _1_ à l'école
d. _5_ au musée

e. _7_ au centre commercial
f. _4_ au restaurant
g. _2_ au lycée
h. _6_ au supermarché

C. Compréhension orale

a. _3_ la bibliothèque
b. _4_ l'hôtel
c. _1_ la piscine
d. _2_ le cinéma

Tu vas au café?

Non, je vais à la plage.

URB
p. 35

Discovering French, Nouveau! Bleu

Unité 5, Leçon 14
Workbook

123

Nom _____

Classe _____ Date _____

D. Questions et réponses

▶ —Est-ce qu'il va au restaurant ou au stade?
  —**Il va au restaurant.**

Elle va à la bibliothèque.

Il va au supermarché.

Ils vont à la plage.

Il va au garage.

E. Questions et réponses

Modèle: le cinéma   —Où vas-tu?
                      —**Je vais au cinéma.**

1. le supermarché *Je vais au supermarché.*
2. la piscine *Je vais à la piscine.*
3. le café *Je vais au café.*

4. la bibliothèque *Je vais à la bibliothèque.*
5. l'école *Je vais à l'école.*

Nom _____

Classe _____ Date _____

Unité 5
Leçon 14
Workbook TE

Discovering FRENCH Nouveau!

BLEU

Section 3. Qu'est-ce que vous allez faire?

F. Compréhension orale

a. _5_   b. _2_   c. _4_   d. _1_   e. _6_

f. _3_   g. _8_   h. _9_   i. _7_

G. Questions et réponses

Modèle: dîner —Tu vas au restaurant?
—Oui, je vais dîner.

1. nager Oui, je vais nager.
2. étudier Oui, je vais étudier.
3. jouer au foot Oui, je vais jouer au foot.
4. faire une promenade Oui, je vais faire une promenade.

5. danser Oui, je vais danser.
6. jouer aux jeux vidéo Oui, je vais jouer aux jeux vidéo.

Section 4. Conversations

H. La réponse logique

1. a. Oui, j'ai faim.
   b. À sept heures.
   c.) Chez un copain.

2. a.) En bus.
   b. À huit heures.
   c. Je vais au restaurant.

3. a. À pied.
   b.) Oui, je vais nager.

   c. Oui, je fais une promenade.

4. a.) Je vais à une boum.
   b. Je fais une omelette.
   c. Oui, d'accord!

5. a. Oui, je vais au concert.
   b. Oui, je vais étudier.
   c.) Oui, je vais au cinéma avec un ami.

6. a. Oui, je vais à un soirée.
   b.) Oui, je vais regarder la télé.
   c. Oui, je fais une promenade.

Nom _____

Classe _____ Date _____

Section 5. Dictée

I. Écoutez et écrivez.

—Vous __restez__ à la maison aujourd'hui?

—Non, nous __allons__ en ville. Moi, je __vais__ aller au cinéma.

—Et ton frère?

—Il a un __rendez-vous__ avec une copine. Ils __vont__ faire une promenade __à pied__ dans le parc municipal.

Nom _____

Classe _____ Date _____

Discovering
FRENCH
Nouveau!

BLEU

Unité 5
Leçon 14
Workbook TE

WRITING ACTIVITIES

A 1. La tour Eiffel

Fit the six forms of **aller** into the Eiffel Tower. Then fill in the blanks to the left with the corresponding subject pronouns.

1. il/elle _____

2. tu _____

3. je _____

4. ils / elles _____

5. vous _____

6. nous _____

V	A
V	A	S
V	A	I	S
V	O	N	T
A	L	L	E	Z
A	L	L	O	N	S

A/B 2. Le week-end

On weekends, people go to different places. Read what the following people like to do. Then say where each one is going by choosing an appropriate place from the list. Use the appropriate forms of **aller à.**

piscine	restaurant	cinéma	musée	stade
plage	bibliothèque	concert	centre commercial	

▶ Caroline aime nager. *Elle va à la piscine.*

1. Philippe et Jean-Louis aiment jouer au football. Ils vont au stade.

2. Mademoiselle Bellamy aime l'art moderne. Elle va au musée.

3. Brigitte aime les westerns. Elle va au cinéma.

4. Paul et Marc aiment la musique. Ils vont au concert.

5. J'aime regarder les magazines français. Je vais à la bibliothèque.

6. Tu aimes dîner en ville. Tu vas au restaurant.

7. Nous aimons nager. Nous allons à la plage (à la piscine).

8. Vous aimez le shopping. Vous allez au centre commercial.

Nom _____

Classe _____ Date _____

B 3. Qu'est-ce qu'ils font?

Describe what the following people are doing. Use the suggested words to form complete sentences.

▶ Jacqueline / parler à / le garçon français

Jacqueline parle au garçon français.

1. Marc / parler à / le professeur

   Marc parle au professeur.

2. Le professeur / parler à / les élèves

   Le professeur parle aux élèves.

3. Le guide / parler à / les touristes

   Le guide parle aux touristes.

4. Nathalie / téléphoner à / le garçon canadien

   Nathalie téléphone au garçon canadien.

5. Hélène / téléphoner à / l'étudiant français

   Hélène téléphone à l'étudiant français.

6. Jean-Pierre / être à / le cinéma

   Jean-Pierre est au cinéma.

7. Juliette / étudier à / la bibliothèque

   Juliette étudie à la bibliothèque.

8. Le taxi / arriver à / l'aéroport

   Le taxi arrive à l'aéroport.

Nom _____

Classe _____ Date _____

Discovering
FRENCH
Nouveau!

BLEU

Unité 5
Leçon 14

Workbook TE

C 4. Les voisins de Mélanie

Mélanie is selling tickets to the school fair and hopes her neighbors will buy some. Indicate that Mélanie is visiting the houses in the illustration. Use the expression **chez.**

▶ Mélanie va *chez Bernard* .

1. Elle va *chez Marie-Claire* .

2. Elle va *chez M. et Mme Berthier* .

3. Elle va *chez le professeur* .

4. Elle va *chez les voisins* .

Discovering French, Nouveau! Bleu

URB
p. 41

Unité 5, Leçon 14
Workbook

129

Nom _____

Classe _____ Date _____

D 5. Qu'est-ce qu'ils vont faire?

The following people are going out. Describe what each one is going to do, using the construction **aller** + infinitive.

▶Je vais faire une promenade à vélo .

1. Nous allons faire une promenade en voiture

2. Vous allez jouer au tennis

3. Tu vas jouer au basket

4. Sylvie va nager

5. M. et Mme Dumaine vont dîner au restaurant

6. Communication: Le week-end (sample answers)

Write a short paragraph about your weekend plans. Describe four things that you are going to do and two things you are not going to do.

OUI!

- Je vais faire une promenade à vélo.

- Je vais téléphoner à mon copain.

- Je vais organiser une boum.

- Je vais regarder la télé.

NON!

- Je ne vais pas jouer au tennis.

- Je ne vais pas aller au cinéma.

Nom _____

Classe _____ Date _____

Discovering FRENCH *Nouveau!*

BLEU

Unité 5
Leçon 14

Unité 5
Leçon 14
Activités pour tous TE

LEÇON 14 Week-end à Paris

A

Activité 1 Allons-y!

Circle the correct forms of **aller** in the dialogues.

1. —Est-ce que nous *vont /* *allons* au cinéma ce soir?
   —Oui, bien sûr.

2. —Chez qui *vais- /* *vas* tu?
   —Je *vais /* vas chez Éric.

3. —Où *vas /* *va* Gilles?
   —Il *vas /* *va* au centre commercial.
   —Moi aussi, je veux *allons /* *aller* aux magasins!

Activité 2 Où vas-tu?

Fill in the blanks with **au** or **à la** to complete the dialogue.

—Tu vas ___au___ stade aujourd'hui?

—Oui, et toi? Tu vas ___à la___ piscine?

—Non, je vais ___à la___ bibliothèque.

—Demain, tu veux aller ___au___ cinéma?

—D'accord! Et après, tu veux aller ___au___ restaurant?

Activité 3 Qu'est-ce qu'ils vont faire demain?

Using the near future **(aller** + infinitive), fill in the blanks to tell or ask what each student is going to do tomorrow. You can look at the box for a reminder of **aller**.

1.
   Patricia
   Elle va étudier.

2.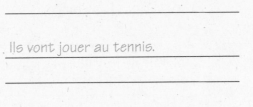
   Des copains
   Ils vont jouer au tennis.

3.
   Vous?
   Est-ce que vous allez nager?

4. Tu?
   Est-ce que tu vas regarder la télé?

5.
   Nous
   Nous allons dîner au restaurant.

Je vais
Tu vas
Il / Elle va
Nous allons
Vous allez
Ils / Elles vont

Nom _____

Classe _____ Date _____

Discovering
FRENCH
Nouveau!

B L E U

B

Activité 1 Dialogues

Match each question with its response, making sure you read both columns first.

_d_ 1.—Où vas-tu?

_e_ 2.—Nous allons au concert maintenant?

_a_ 3.—Tu étudies? Tu peux jouer avec moi?

_b_ 4.—Maman, je peux aller chez ma copine?

_c_ 5.—Vous allez au stade?

a. —Non, va-t-en, s'il te plaît. Je prépare un examen.

b. —Oui, vas-y!

c. —Oui, nous allons jouer au foot.

d. —Je vais à la bibliothèque.

e. —Oui, allons-y!

Activité 2 Où allez-vous?

Fill in the blanks with **à, au, à la, à l'** or **aux** to complete these sentences.

1. Nous n'allons pas _à l'_ école le samedi.

2. Je vais aller _à_ Paris.

3. Est-ce que tu veux aller _à la_ boum?

4. Nous dînons souvent _au_ restaurant.

5. Tu vas _au_ parc _à_ vélo ou _à_ pied?

Activité 3 Le futur immédiat

Transform these sentences using **aller** + infinitive. You can look at the box for a reminder of **aller**.

Je vais	Nous allons	Il/Elle va
Tu vas	Vous allez	Ils/Elles vont

1. Ils jouent au foot.

   Ils vont jouer au foot.

2. Nous étudions à la bibliothèque.

   Nous allons étudier à la bibliothèque.

3. Tu es chez toi.

   Tu vas être chez toi.

4. Je vais chez Michèle.

   Je vais aller chez Michèle.

5. Elle ne travaille pas aujourd'hui.

   Elle ne va pas travailler aujourd'hui.

6. Est-ce que vous mangez au restaurant?

   Est-ce que vous allez manger au restaurant?

Nom _____

Classe _____ Date _____

C

Activité 1 Où vont-ils? (sample answers)

Use the agenda below to ask four questions about where these people go every week on specific days.

Modèle: Le lundi, est-ce que tu vas au stade?

lundi	mardi	mercredi	jeudi	vendredi	samedi	dimanche
Tu	Yves	Les enfants	Sabine	Ta famille et toi	Steve et Natasha	Ta famille

1. Le mardi, est-ce que Yves va à la bibliothèque? _____

2. Le mercredi, est-ce que les enfants vont au parc? _____

3. Le jeudi, est-ce que Sabine va à la piscine? _____

4. Le vendredi, est-ce que vous allez au cinéma? _____

Activité 2 Une semaine à Paris

You are going to Paris for a week and you are planning to do a million things there! Complete the paragraph about some of your activities, with **à** or the appropriate contraction.

Quand j'arrive _à___ Paris mardi, je vais aller _à___ l'hôtel

immédiatement. Après, je vais faire une promenade _aux___ Champs-Élysées.

Mercredi, je vais aller _au___ musée d'Orsay et _à la___ Bibliothèque

Nationale. Jeudi, je vais aller _au___ centre commercial en métro. Vendredi, je

vais aller _à la___ piscine municipale. Samedi, je vais aller _au___ stade pour

regarder un match de foot.

Activité 3 Des résolutions

It's New Year's and you are describing to your French pen pal your family's resolutions for the year ahead. Using the cues provided, make complete sentences with **aller.**

1. Je _vais étudier_____

2. Ma soeur _va jouer_____ au tennis_____

3. Mes cousins _vont_____ chanter_____

4. Mon frère _va_____ travailler_____

5. Nous _allons_____ voyager_____

LEÇON 14 Week-end à Paris, page 204

Objectives

Communicative Functions and Topics
To talk about how you get around and modes of transportation
To describe places you often go to
To talk about going to someone's house
To tell what you are going to do

Linguistic Goals
To use the verb *aller* and *aller* + infinitive
To use contractions with *à*
To pronounce semi-vowels /w/ and /j/
To learn the expression *chez*

Cultural Goals
To learn about attractions in Paris and the *métro*

Motivation and Focus

❏ Have students discuss the photos on pages 204–205. Ask them to name their favorite weekend activities and places to visit. Discuss similarities and differences between Paris and local attractions. Share the NOTE CULTURELLE, page 205 of the TE.

Presentation and Explanation

❏ *Lesson Opener:* Play **Audio CD** 3, Tracks 4–5 or read the opening monologue with students' books closed. Ask students to read page 204 and make a list of the people and the places they go.

❏ *Note culturelle:* Ask students to read *À Paris* on page 205 to find out about some of the places where young people might go on weekends in Paris.

❏ *Grammar A:* Present *aller*, page 206. Model the forms and examples; have students repeat. Explain that *aller* can be used for going someplace or for future activities.

❏ *Grammar B:* Call attention to the preposition *à* and contractions, page 208. Point out the various meanings of *à* and the forms of the contractions.

❏ *Vocabulaire:* Introduce means of transportation using the pictures on **Overhead Transparency** 33. Model and have students repeat the expressions in the box on page 210. Guide students to talk about places they go, arrival times, and transportation.

❏ *Grammar C:* Explain the use of *chez*, page 211; have students practice talking about going to someone's house. Explain the PRONUNCIATION note, page 211 of the TE.

❏ *Grammar D:* Introduce the construction *aller* + infinitive, page 212. Model talking about future plans and help students talk about their own plans for the future.

❏ *Prononciation:* Explain semi-vowels, page 213. Model or use **Audio CD** 3, Track 6 to model pronunciation and have students repeat.

Guided Practice and Checking Understanding

❏ Use **Overhead Transparency** 33 and the activities on page A95 to practice means of transportation and contractions.

❏ Play **Audio CD** 9, Tracks 8–16 or read the **Audioscript**, and have students do **Workbook** Listening Activities A–I on pages 123–126.

❏ Use the **Video** or **Videoscript** as students do **Video Activities** pages 56–60.

❏ Do the COMPREHENSION ACTIVITY on page 205 of the TE to practice names of places in Paris.

Independent Practice

❏ Do the Activities on pages 206–213. Students can work alone on 1, 2, and 6–10. Arrange students in pairs to do 3–5, 7, and 11 as PAIR PRACTICE. Have students do Activity 12 as homework.

❏ Use **Communipak** for *Conversations* 5–8, pages 147–148; *Échanges* 1–2, pages 149–150; or *Tête à tête* 2, pages 155–156. Do **Video Activities** page 61 to role play brief conversations on the *métro*.

❏ Have students do the activities in **Activités pour tous,** pages 75–77.

Monitoring and Adjusting

❏ Assign Writing Activities 1–6 on **Workbook** pages 127–130.

❏ Monitor students as they work on the practice activities. Point out grammar boxes, pages 206–213. Use the TEACHING NOTE: LISTENING ACTIVITIES on page 206 of the TE, and the ADDITIONAL PRACTICE drill at the bottom of page 208 of the TE.

Assessment

❏ After students have completed all of the lesson's activities, administer Quiz 14 on pages 69–70. Adapt questions to meet your needs using the **Test Generator**.

Reteaching

❏ Redo any of activities in the **Workbook** for which students need more practice.

❏ Have students do **Teacher to Teacher** pages 13 and 14.

❏ Students can use the **Video** to review portions of the lesson.

Extension and Enrichment

❏ Share information about other Paris attractions with CULTURAL BACKGROUND: L'OPÉRA, page 209 of the TE; and CULTURAL NOTES, page 212 of the TE. If students are interested, have them prepare a research project on one of the attractions.

❏ Play the GAME on page 213 of the TE.

Summary and Closure

❏ Choose one of the lesson's **Communipak** activities that students did not previously do. Have students prepare and practice the exchanges. After students present their work to the class, remind them of the grammar and vocabulary they have learned in the lesson.

❏ Do PORTFOLIO ASSESSMENT on page 214 of the TE.

End-of-Lesson Activities

❏ *À votre tour!:* Students can prepare and practice Activities 1–3, pages 214 and 215. Use **Audio CD** 3, Tracks 7–8 with Activities 1–2. Assign Activities 4 and 5 for written homework. Follow the suggestions at the bottom of page 215 of the TE for GROUP READING AND WRITING PRACTICE.

Unité 5
Leçon 14

Block Scheduling
Lesson Plans

Discovering
FRENCH
Nouveau!

BLEU

LEÇON 14 Week-end à Paris, page 204

Block Scheduling (3 days to complete)

Objectives

Communicative Functions and Topics To talk about how you get around and modes of transportation
To describe places you often go to
To talk about going to someone's house
To tell what you are going to do

Linguistic Goals To use the verb *aller* and *aller* + infinitive
To use contractions with *à*
To pronounce semi-vowels /w/ and /j/
To learn the expression *chez*

Cultural Goals To learn about attractions in Paris and the *métro*

Day 1

Motivation and Focus

❑ Have students discuss the photos on pages 204–205. Ask them to name their favorite weekend activities and places to visit. Discuss similarities and differences between Paris and local attractions. Share the NOTE CULTURELLE, page 205 of the TE.

Presentation and Explanation

❑ *Lesson Opener:* Play **Audio CD** 3, Track 4–5, or read the opening monologue with students' books closed. Ask students to read page 204 and make a list of the people and the places they go.

❑ *Note culturelle:* Ask students to read *À Paris* on page 205 to find out about some of the places where young people might go on weekends in Paris.

❑ *Grammar A:* Present *aller*, page 206. Model the forms and examples; have students repeat. Explain that *aller* can be used for going someplace or for future activities.

❑ *Grammar B:* Call attention to the preposition *à* and contractions, page 208. Point out the various meanings of *à* and the forms of the contractions.

❑ *Vocabulaire:* Introduce means of transportation using the pictures on **Overhead Transparency** 33. Model and have students repeat the expressions in the box on page 210. Guide students to talk about places they go, arrival times, and transportation.

❑ *Grammar C:* Explain the use of *chez*, page 211; have students practice talking about going to someone's house. Explain the PRONUNCIATION NOTE, page 211 of the TE.

❑ *Grammar D:* Introduce the construction *aller* + infinitive, page 212. Model talking about future plans and help students talk about their own plans for the future.

❑ *Prononciation:* Explain semi-vowels, page 213. Model or use **Audio CD** 3, Track 6 to model pronunciation and have students repeat.

Guided Practice and Checking Understanding

❑ Use **Overhead Transparency** 33 and the activities on page A95 to practice means of transportation and contractions.

❑ Play **Audio CD** 9, Tracks 8–16 or read the **Audioscript**, and have students do **Workbook** Listening Activities A–I on pages 123–126.

Discovering
FRENCH *Nouveau!*

BLEU

Unité 5
Leçon 14
Block Scheduling
Lesson Plans

Day 2

Motivation and Focus

❑ Use the **Video** or **Videoscript** as students do **Video Activities** pages 56–60.
❑ Do the COMPREHENSION ACTIVITY on page 205 of the TE to practice names of places in Paris.

Independent Practice

❑ Do the activities on pages 206–213. Students can work alone on 1, 2, and 6–10. Arrange students in pairs to do 3–5, 7, and 11 as PAIR PRACTICE. Have students do Activity 12 as homework.
❑ Use **Communipak** for *Conversations* 5–8, pages 147–148; *Échanges* 1–2, pages 149–150; or *Tête à tête* 2, pages 155–156. Do **Video Activities** page 61 to role play brief conversations on the *métro*.
❑ Use **Block Scheduling Copymasters,** pages 105–112.

Monitoring and Adjusting

❑ Assign Writing Activities 1–6 on **Workbook** pages 127–130.
❑ Monitor students as they work on the practice activities. Point out grammar boxes, pages 206–213. Use the TEACHING NOTE: LISTENING ACTIVITIES on page 206 of the TE, and the ADDITIONAL PRACTICE drill at the bottom of page 208 of the TE.

Day 3

End-of-Lesson Activities

❑ *À votre tour!:* Students can prepare and practice Activities 1–3, pages 214 and 215. Use **Audio CD** 3, Tracks 7–8 with Activities 1–2. Assign Activities 4 and 5 for written homework. Follow suggestions on page 215 of the TE for GROUP READING AND WRITING PRACTICE.

Reteaching (as needed)

❑ Redo any of the activities in the **Workbook** for which students need more practice.
❑ Have students do **Teacher to Teacher** pages 13 and 14.
❑ Students can use the **Video** to review portions of the lesson.

Extension and Enrichment (as desired)

❑ Share information about other Paris attractions with CULTURAL BACKGROUND: L'OPÉRA, page 209 of the TE; and CULTURAL NOTES, page 212 of the TE. If students are interested, have them prepare a research project on one of the attractions.
❑ Play the GAME on page 213 of the TE.
❑ For expansion activities, direct students to www.classzone.com.

Summary and Closure

❑ Choose one of the lesson's **Communipak** activities that students did not previously do. Have students prepare and practice the exchanges. After students present their work to the class, remind them of the grammar and vocabulary they have learned in the lesson.
❑ Do PORTFOLIO ASSESSMENT on page 214 of the TE.

Assessment

❑ After students have completed all of the lesson's activities, administer Quiz 14 on pages 69–70. Adapt questions to meet your needs using the **Test Generator.**

Nom _____

Classe _____ Date _____

Discovering
FRENCH
Nouveau!

B L E U

LEÇON 14 Week-end à Paris, pages 204–205

Materials Checklist

- **Student Text**
- **Audio CD** 3, Tracks 4–5
- **Video** 3 or **DVD** 2; Counter 7:47–14:09

Steps to Follow

- Read *Week-end à Paris* (p. 204). Look at the pictures.
- Before listening to the audio or watching the video, read the *Compréhension* questions (p. 205). They will help you understand what you hear.
- Watch **Video** 3 or **DVD** 2; Counter 7:47–14:09, or listen to **Audio CD** 3, Tracks 4–5.
- Answer the *Compréhension* questions (p. 205) in complete sentences on a separate sheet of paper.
- Read the *Note culturelle* and look at the photos on p. 205.

If You Don't Understand . . .

- Watch the **Video** or **DVD** in a quiet place. Try to stay focused. If you get lost, stop the **Video** or **DVD**. Replay it and find your place.
- Listen to the **CD** in a quiet place. Try to stay focused. If you get lost, stop the **CD**. Replay it and find your place.
- Repeat aloud with the audio. Try to sound like the people on the recording.
- On a separate sheet of paper, write down the words that are underlined in the text. Check for meaning.

Self-Check

Answer the following questions on a separate sheet of paper. Write complete sentences.

1. Est-ce que les Champs-Élysées sont une avenue longue et large?
2. Est-ce que le Centre Pompidou est un stade?
3. Est-ce que le Parc de la Villette est un centre commercial?
4. Es-ce que Paris offre beaucoup d'attractions?

Answers

1. **Oui**, les Champs-Élysées sont une avenue longue et large. 2. **Non**, le Centre Pompidou est un musée. 3. **Non**, le Parc de la Villette est un musée scientifique. 4. **Oui**, Paris offre beaucoup d'attractions.

Nom _____

Classe _____ Date _____ _____

Discovering
FRENCH *Nouveau!*

B L E U

Unité 5
Leçon 14

Absent Student Copymasters

A. Le verbe *aller,* pages 206–207

Materials Checklist

- **Student Text**
- **Audio CD** 9, Track 8
- **Workbook**

Steps to Follow

- Study *Le verbe* **aller** (p. 206). Copy the conjugation and read it aloud.
- Study the pictures showing the use of common expressions with **aller** (p. 206).
- Complete Activities 1 and 2 in the text (p. 207). Write your answers in complete sentences on a separate sheet of paper. Underline the different forms of **aller**.
- Do **Writing Activities** A 1 and A/B 2 in the **Workbook** (p. 127).
- Do **Listening Activities** A in the **Workbook** (p. 123). Use **Audio CD** 9, Track 8.

If You Don't Understand . . .

- Listen to the **CD** in a quiet place. Try to stay focused. If you get lost, stop the **CD**. Replay it and find your place.
- Reread the activity directions. Put the directions in your own words.
- Say aloud everything that you write. Be sure you understand what you are saying.
- Write down questions so that you can ask your partner or your teacher later.
- When writing a sentence, ask yourself, "What do I mean? What am I trying to say?"

Self-Check

Answer the following questions on a separate sheet of paper. Use the appropriate pronoun, and write complete sentences.

1. Où va Philippe? (au restaurant)
2. Où vont Thomas et Annette? (à un concert)
3. Où vas-tu? (à la plage)
4. Où allons-nous? (au stade)
5. Où allez-vous? (en ville)
6. Où va Jeanne? (au café)

Answers

5. Nous allons en ville. / Je vais en ville.   6. Elle va au café.

1. Il va au restaurant.   2. Ils vont à un concert.   3. Je vais à la plage.   4. Nous allons au stade.

Discovering
FRENCH
Nouveau!

BLEU

Nom _____

Classe _____ Date _____

B. La préposition *à*; *à* + l'article défini, pages 208–210

Materials Checklist

- **Student Text**
- **Audio CD** 9, Tracks 9–12
- **Video** 3 or **DVD** 2; Counter 7:47–14:09
- **Workbook**

Steps to Follow

- Study *La préposition à; à + l'article défini* (p. 208).
- Write the singular and plural forms of **à** and the definite article. Underline the contractions.
- Watch **Video** 3 or **DVD** 2; Counter 7:47–14:09.
- Do Activity 3 (p. 208). Write the question and the answer for each picture. Read them aloud.
- Do Activity 4 (p. 209). Write the parts for both speakers.
- Do Activities 5 and 6 (p. 209). Write the answers on a separate sheet.
- Study *Vocabulaire: En ville* (p. 210). Write the vocabulary on a separate sheet of paper.
- Do Activity 7 (p. 210). Underline the new expressions, for example, **En général, j'arrive à l'école à 9 heures.**
- Do **Writing Activities** B 3 in the **Workbook** (p. 128).
- Do **Listening Activities** B–E in the **Workbook** (pp. 123–124). Use **Audio CD** 9, Tracks 9–12.

If You Don't Understand . . .

- Watch the **Video** or **DVD** in a quiet place. Try to stay focused. If you get lost, stop the **Video** or **DVD**. Replay it and find your place.
- Listen to the **CD** in a quiet place. Try to stay focused. If you get lost, stop the **CD**. Replay it and find your place.
- Reread the activity directions. Put the directions in your own words.
- Read the model several times. Be sure you understand it.
- Say aloud everything that you write. Be sure you understand what you are saying.
- Write down questions so that you can ask your partner or your teacher later.

Self-Check

Answer the following questions on a separate sheet of paper. Use the appropriate pronoun, and write complete sentences.

1. Où vas-tu? (l'Opéra)
2. Où allons-nous samedi? (le cinéma)
3. Où allez-vous ce week-end? (la piscine)
4. Où est-ce que Jean et Alain vont demain matin? (le café)
5. Où va Hélène? (les Champs-Élysées)

Answers

1. Je vais à l'Opéra. 2. Nous allons au cinéma. 3. Je vais à la piscine. / Nous allons à la piscine. 4. Ils vont au café. 5. Elle va aux Champs-Élysées.

Nom _____

Classe _____ Date _____

Discovering
FRENCH
Nouveau!

BLEU

Unité 5
Leçon 14

Absent Student Copymasters

C. La préposition *chez;* page 211
D. La construction *aller* + l'infinitif, pages 212–213

Materials Checklist

- **Student Text**
- **Audio CD** 3, Tracks 6–8; **CD** 9, Tracks 13–16
- **Video** 3 or **DVD** 2; Counter 9:42–12:40
- **Workbook**

Steps to Follow

- Study *La préposition chez* (p. 211). Say the model sentences aloud. Copy the models on a separate sheet of paper.
- Review the conjugation of **aller** (p. 206). Do activities 8 and 9 in the text (p. 211).
- Study *La construction aller + l'infinitif* (p. 212). Say the model sentences aloud. Copy the models on a separate sheet of paper.
- Watch **Video** 3 or **DVD** 2; Counter 9:42–12:40. Repeat what you hear.
- Do Activity 10 in the text (p. 212). Write the answers on a separate sheet.
- Do Activities 11 and 12 in the text (p. 213).
- Read the list of words in *Prononciation: Les semi-voyelles /w/ and /j/* (p. 213). Listen to *Prononciation: Les semi-voyelles /w/* and */j/* on **Audio CD** 3, Track 6. Repeat what you hear.
- Do **Writing Activities** C 4 and D 5, 6 in the **Workbook** (pp. 129–130).
- Do **Listening Activities** F–I in the **Workbook** (pp. 125–126). Use **Audio CD** 9, Tracks 13–16.
- Do Activities 1–5 of *À votre tour!* in the text (pp. 214–215). Use **Audio CD** 3, Tracks 7–8 with Activities 1 and 2.

If You Don't Understand

- Reread the activity directions. Put the directions in your own words.
- Read the model several times before beginning. Be sure you understand it. Copy the model.
- Write down any questions so that you can ask your teacher or your partner later.
- Watch the **Video** or **DVD** in a quiet place. Try to stay focused. If you get lost, stop the **Video** or **DVD**. Replay it and find your place.
- Listen to the **CDs** in a quiet place. Try to stay focused. If you get lost, stop the **CDs**. Replay them and find your place. Repeat aloud with the audio. Try to sound like the people on the recording.

Self-Check

Using the following expressions, tell what each person is going to do this weekend. Write complete sentences on a separate sheet of paper.

1. Je / travailler / chez Jean
2. Alice / visiter / le Louvre
3. Nous / jouer / au basket
4. Vous / faire une promenade
5. Ils / aller / au cinéma

Answers

1. Je vais travailler chez Jean. 2. Alice va visiter le Louvre. 3. Nous allons jouer au basket. 4. Vous allez faire une promenade. 5. Ils vont aller au cinéma.

URB
p. 53

Nom _____

Classe _____ Date _____

LEÇON 14 Week-end à Paris

Comment vas-tu à . . . ?

Ask a family member about how he or she goes to work (**le travail**) or to school.

• First, explain your assignment.
• Model the pronunciation of the words below the pictures. Point to the picture as you model each answer.
• Ask the question: **Comment vas-tu au travail / à l'école?**
• When you have an answer, complete the sentence at the bottom of the page.

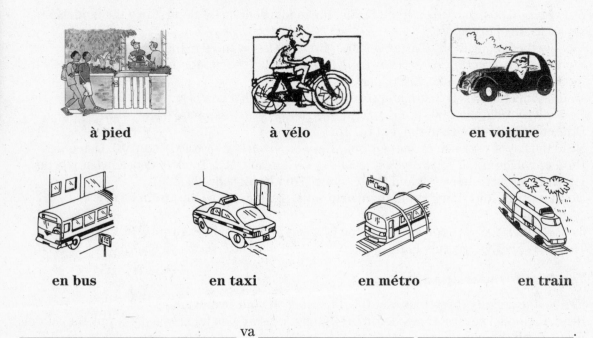

à pied   à vélo   en voiture

en bus   en taxi   en métro   en train

_____ va _____ _____.

Nom _____

Classe _____ Date _____

Un endroit intéressant

Ask a family member to imagine that he or she is *going to go* to one of the following places. Have him or her pick the most interesting one.

- First, explain your assignment.
- Help him or her pronounce the names of the places correctly by modeling the pronunciation. Point to the picture as you model each answer.
- Then, ask him or her the question: **Où vas-tu aller?**
- After you get an answer, complete the sentence at the bottom of the page.

au cinéma

à la bibliothèque

au musée

à la plage

_____ va aller _____ .

Nom _____

Classe _____ Date _____

MODULE 14 Une promenade en ville

Video 3, DVD 2

14.1 Activité 1. En ville   Counter 7:47–8:20

Listen as various people on the video tell you where
they are going. Circle the letter of the correct
completion to each statement below. The sentences
are given in the order you hear them on the video.

1. Je vais …	a. au théâtre	b. à l'école
2. Nous allons …	a. au lycée	b. au musée
3. Je vais …	a. à l'école	b. au café
4. Nous allons …	a. au restaurant	b. au théâtre
5. Je vais …	a. au musée	b. à la piscine
6. Je vais …	a. au restaurant	b. au supermarché
7. Je vais …	a. à l'école	b. au centre commercial
8. Nous allons …	a. au café	b. au stade
9. Je vais …	a. chez une copine	b. chez Claire

14.2 Activité 2. Où allez-vous?   Counter 8:21–8:46

Where are each of the five people in the video off to? As you watch, circle the letter of the
correct destination for each person.

1. **Nathalie**
   a. à la piscine
   b. à l'école

2. **Sandrine**
   a. chez un copain
   b. chez une copine

3. **Stéphanie**
   a. au cinéma
   b. au café

4. **la jeune fille**
   a. à la plage
   b. à la bibliothèque

5. **la dame**
   a. à l'hôpital
   b. à l'hôtel

Nom _____

Classe _____ Date _____

Discovering FRENCH *Nouveau!*

B L E U

Unité 5
Leçon 14
Video Activities

14.3 **Activité 3.** Où vont-ils?

More people are going places! After you watch the video segment, draw a line from each sentence to the picture of the corresponding destination.

a.

1. Il va au restaurant.

2. Elle va à la bibliothèque.

3. Elle va au supermarché.

4. Ils vont à la plage.

5. Il va au garage.

e.

d.

b.

c.

Nom _____

Classe _____ Date _____

14.4 Activité 4. Qu'est-ce que vous allez faire?

Counter 9:42–11:00

Watch the video, and then number the captions in the order in which you hear them, starting with 1 and ending with 6.

a. _____ **Je vais faire une promenade.**

d. _____ **Je vais jouer au tennis.**

b. _____ **Nous allons nager.**

e. _____ **Nous allons jouer au volley.**

c. _____ **Je vais travailler.**

f. _____ **Je vais téléphoner.**

14.4 Activité 5. Endroits et activités

Counter 7:47–8:20

People are going different places and are doing different things. Watch the video and fill in each blank below with the appropriate word from the box.

jouer au foot	dîner	regarder la télé
visiter	étudier	jouer aux jeux vidéo

1. Nous allons au restaurant. Nous allons _____.

2. Nous allons _____ le musée d'Orsay.

3. Je vais au stade. Je vais _____.

4. Je vais chez une copine. Nous allons _____.

5. Je vais dans ma chambre. Je vais _____.

6. Je vais à la bibliothèque. Je vais _____.

Nom _____

Classe _____ Date _____

14.5 Activité 6. Tu vas nager?

Counter 11:01–11:49

What are you going to do this weekend? After you watch the video segment, look at the pictures and fill in the blank in each question with the appropriate word or phrase from the box.

organiser une boum	**jouer au tennis**
étudier **nager**	**dîner au restaurant**

1. Tu vas _____?

2. Tu vas _____?

3. Tu vas _____?

4. Tu vas _____?

5. Tu vas _____?

Nom _____

Classe _____ Date _____

Discovering
FRENCH
Nouveau!

B L E U

14.6 Activité 7. Où va Julien?

Why must Julien suddenly leave his friends at the café? Circle the letter of the correct completion to the statements below.

1. Julien va . . .   a. à l'école   b. à la maison   c. à la piscine

2. Il va . . .   a. étudier   b. nager   c. travailler

14.7 Activité 8. Le métro

As you watch the **Vignette culturelle**, decide whether the statements below are true or false. Mark an **X** in the appropriate column.

	vrai	faux
1. In France, public transportation is inexpensive.	❑	❑
2. **Le métro** is the name of the Paris subway system.	❑	❑
3. It is necessary to buy **un ticket** to ride the **métro**.	❑	❑
4. A book of tickets is called **un carnet**.	❑	❑
5. Passengers have their tickets validated on the platform.	❑	❑

Question personnelle: If you visit Paris, would you like to ride the **métro**? Why or why not?

Réponse: _____

Nom _____

Classe _____ Date _____

Discovering
FRENCH
Nouveau!

B L E U

Unité 5
Leçon 14
Video Activities

 ### Activité 9. En métro

With a classmate, pretend you are on the **métro**. You have just bumped into your classmate and one of you starts a conversation. You both takes turns asking and answering questions about how each of you is feeling, where you are going, and what you will do when you get there. Then end your conversation with a good-bye.

▶ ÉLÈVE 1: **Salut! Ça va?**

ÉLÈVE 2: **Oui, ça va. Et toi?**

ÉLÈVE 1: **Ça va. Où est-ce que tu vas?**

ÉLÈVE 2: **Je vais . . . etc.**

Discovering
FRENCH
Nouveau!

BLEU

MODULE 14   Une promenade en ville

There are many things we can do when we go downtown. We can go shopping. We can go to the movies or to a café. Or we can simply walk along the streets and through the parks.

Video 3, DVD 2

14.1 Mini-scenes: Listening—Où allez-vous?   Counter 7:47–8:20

Let's find out where people are going.
Où allez-vous?

—Je vais à l'école.
—Nous allons au lycée.
—Je vais au café.
—Nous allons au restaurant.
—Je vais au musée.
—Je vais au supermarché.
—Je vais au centre commercial.
—Nous allons au stade.
—Je vais chez une copine.

14.2 Mini-scenes: Listening—Où est-ce que tu vas?   Counter 8:21–8:46

Now listen to these conversations.

—Où vas-tu?
—Je vais à la piscine. Et toi?
—Moi, je vais chez un copain.
—Salut!
—Salut!

—Ça va?
—Oui, ça va.
—Tu vas où?
—Je vais au cinéma.

—Où est-ce que tu vas?
—Je vais à la bibliothèque.

—Hep, taxi!
—Où allez-vous, madame?
—Je vais à l'hôtel Méridien.

14.3 Mini-scenes: Speaking—Où vont-ils?   Counter 8:47–9:41

Now it's your turn to speak. Look at the illustrations and say where each person is going.

—Est-ce qu'il va au restaurant ou au stade? [screen card]
—Il va au restaurant.

—Est-ce qu'elle va au supermarché ou à la bibliothèque? [screen card]
—Elle va à la bibliothèque.

—Est-ce qu'il va au cinéma ou au supermarché? [screen card]
—Il va au supermarché.

—Est-ce qu'ils vont à la plage ou à l'école? [screen card]
—Ils vont à la plage.

—Est-ce qu'il va au garage ou à l'hôpital? [screen card]
—Il va au garage.

14.4 Mini-scenes: Listening—Qu'est-ce que vous allez faire?   Counter 9:42–11:00

Now we'll ask people what they're going to do. Listen carefully to how they answer the question: ***Qu'est-ce que vous allez faire?***

Qu'est-ce que vous allez faire?

—Je vais jouer au tennis.
—Je vais faire une promenade.
—Nous allons jouer au volley.
—Je vais travailler.
—Nous allons nager.
—Je vais téléphoner.

Now watch the following conversations.

—Salut!
—Salut!
—Qu'est-ce que vous allez faire?
—Nous allons dîner.

—Et vous, qu'est-ce que vous allez faire?
—Nous allons visiter le musée d'Orsay.

—Où est-ce que tu vas?
—Je vais au stade.

—Qu'est-ce que tu vas faire?
—Ben . . . je vais jouer au foot.

—Salut, Céline! Où est-ce que tu vas?
—Je vais chez une copine.
—Ah, bon? Et qu'est-ce que vous allez faire?
—Nous allons jouer aux jeux vidéo.
—Alors, salut!
—Salut!

—Où est-ce que tu vas?
—Dans ma chambre.
—Qu'est-ce que tu vas faire?
—Je vais regarder la télé.

—Bonjour.
—Bonjour.
—Où est-ce que tu vas?
—Je vais à la bibliothèque.
—Qu'est-ce que tu vas faire?
—Je vais étudier.
—Salut.
—Salut.

14.5 Mini-scenes: Speaking—Tu vas nager?

Counter 11:01–11:49

It's your turn to speak again. You'll be asked if you're going to do certain things this weekend. Answer either yes or no.

—Tu vas nager?
—Oui, je vais nager.
—Et toi?
—Non, je ne vais pas nager.

—Tu vas étudier? [Oui, je vais étudier./
Non, je ne vais pas étudier.]

—Tu vas jouer au tennis? [Oui, je vais jouer au tennis./
Non, je ne vais pas jouer au tennis.]

—Tu vas dîner au restaurant? [Oui, je vais dîner au restaurant./
Non, je ne vais pas dîner au restaurant.]

—Tu vas organiser une boum? [Oui, je vais organiser une boum./
Non, je ne vais pas organiser une boum.]

14.6 Dialogue: Julien travaille

Counter 11:50–12:40

Julien must suddenly leave his friends at a café. Let's find out why.

OLIVIER: Tu restes avec nous?
JULIEN: Je ne peux pas.
CLAIRE: Où vas-tu?
JULIEN: Je vais à la piscine.
CLAIRE: Ah bon? Tu vas nager?
JULIEN: Non, je vais travailler.
VALÉRIE: Tu vas travailler? Tu plaisantes!
JULIEN: Mais non! Allez, salut!
OLIVIER: Salut!

OLIVIER: Dis, Julien! mais qu'est-ce que tu fais là?
JULIEN: Ben, tu vois. Je travaille!

14.7 Vignette culturelle: Le métro

Counter 12:41–14:09

*If you were on a trip to France, how would you get around in the city you were visiting? Depending on the city you are in, you could walk, take a taxi, a bus, or a subway. In France, public transportation is efficient, fast, and inexpensive. In Paris, you can take the subway, **le métro**, to go almost anywhere in the city or suburbs. Let's take a **métro** ride with Anne.*

*First, Anne buys a ticket, **un ticket**.*

ANNE: Je voudrais un ticket de métro.

*You can also buy a book of tickets called **un carnet**, if you plan to use the **métro** several times. She needs to have her ticket validated before going to the platform: this is called **composter le ticket**. In the **métro**, you never have long to wait—trains come at regular intervals. The doors open automatically and Anne finds a seat and enjoys her ride on the **métro**!*

Discovering
FRENCH
Nouveau!

BLEU

LEÇON 14 Week-end à Paris

PE AUDIO

CD 3, Track 4

Compréhension orale, p. 204

Aujourd'hui c'est samedi.
Les élèves ne vont pas en classe.
Où est-ce qu'ils vont alors?
Ça dépend!

Thomas va au café.
Il a un rendez-vous avec une copine.

Florence et Karine vont aux Champs-
Élysées.
Elles vont regarder les vêtements dans les
magasins.
Après, elles vont aller au cinéma.

Daniel va chez son copain Laurent.
Les garçons vont jouer aux jeux vidéo.
Après, ils vont aller au musée des sciences
de la Villette.
Ils vont jouer avec les machines
électroniques.

Béatrice a un grand sac et des lunettes de
soleil.
Est-ce qu'elle va à un rendez-vous secret?
Non! Elle va au Centre Pompidou.
Elle va regarder les acrobates.
Et après, elle va écouter un concert.

Et Jean-François? Qu'est-ce qu'il va faire
aujourd'hui?
Est-ce qu'il va visiter le Centre Pompidou?
Est-ce qu'il va regarder les acrobates?
Est-ce qu'il va écouter un concert?
Hélas, non!
Il va rester à la maison.
Pourquoi? Parce qu'il est malade.
Pauvre Jean-François!
Il fait si beau dehors!

CD 3, Track 5

Écoutez et répétez., p. 204

You will now hear a paused version of the
dialogue. Listen to the speaker and repeat right
after he or she has completed the sentence.

Prononciation, p. 213

CD 3, Track 6

Les semi-voyelles /w/ et /j/

Écoutez. oui   très bien

In French, the semi-vowels /w/ and /j/ are
pronounced very quickly, almost like
consonants.

Répétez: /w/ #   oui # chouette #
                              Louise #
              /wa/, /wɛ̃/ # moi # toi # pourquoi #
                              voiture # loin #
Chouette! La voiture de Louise
   n'est pas loin. #
              /j/   # bien # chien # radio
                              # piano # Pierre #
                              Daniel # violon # pied
                              # étudiant #

Pierre écoute la radio avec Daniel. #

A votre tour!

CD 3, Track 7

1. Allô!, p. 214

Listen to the phone conversation. *Écoutez la
conversation entre Anne et Jérôme.*

ANNE: Tu restes chez toi samedi?
JÉRÔME: Non, j'ai un rendez-vous avec
        Christine.
ANNE: Qu'est-ce que vous allez faire?
JÉRÔME: Nous allons faire une promenade
        en ville.
ANNE: Est-ce que vous allez aller au
        cinéma?

JÉRÔME: Peut-être! Il y a un très bon film au Rex.

ANNE: À quelle heure est-ce que tu vas rentrer?

JÉRÔME: À dix heures.

CD 3, Track 8

2. Créa-dialogue, p. 214

Listen to some sample *Créa-dialogues*. *Écoutez les conversations.*

Modèle: —Salut, Alison. Ça va?
—Oui, ça va!
—Où vas-tu?
—Je vais au restaurant.

—Ah bon? Qu'est-ce que tu vas faire là-bas?
—Je vais dîner avec un copain.
—Avec qui?
—Avec Chris.

Maintenant, écoutez le dialogue numéro 1.

—Salut Tom.
—Ça va?
—Oui, ça va!
—Où vas-tu?
—Je vais au café.
—Ah bon? Qu'est-ce que tu vas faire là-bas?
—Je vais manger une pizza.
—Avec qui?
—Avec Sally.

WORKBOOK AUDIO

Section 1. Je vais à . . .

CD 9, Track 8

A. Écoutez et répétez., p. 123

You will hear sentences containing forms of the verb "aller." Listen and repeat where different people are going.

1. Je vais en classe. #
2. Tu vas au café. #
3. Il va au cinéma. #
4. Nous allons à une boum. #
5. Vous allez à Paris. #
6. Ils vont en France. #

Section 2. Où vont-ils?

CD 9, Track 9

B. Compréhension orale, p. 123

Listen as various people are asked where they are going. Listen to their answers. Then, in your Workbook, write the corresponding number next to the place they mention.

Modèle: 1. —Où allez-vous?
—Je vais à l'école.

You would write the number "1" next to item "c": l'école.

2. —Où allez-vous?
—Nous allons au lycée. #

3. —Où allez-vous?
—Je vais au café. #

4. —Où allez-vous?
—Nous allons au restaurant. #

5. —Où allez-vous?
—Je vais au musée. #

6. —Où allez-vous?
—Je vais au supermarché. #

7. —Où allez-vous?
—Je vais au centre commercial. #

8. —Où allez-vous?
—Nous allons au stade. #

Now check your answers. You should have matched the conversations with the places as follows: a-8, b-3, c-1, d-5, e-7, f-4, g-2, and h-6.

CD 9, Track 10

C. Compréhension orale, p. 123

Now you will hear four different conversations. Again write the corresponding number next to the place mentioned.

1. —Où vas-tu?
   —Je vais à la piscine. Et toi?
   —Moi, je vais chez un copain.
   —Salut!
   —Salut! #

2. —Ça va?
   —Oui, ça va.
   —Tu vas où?
   —Je vais au cinéma. #

3. —Où est-ce que tu vas?
   —Je vais à la bibliothèque. #

4. —Hep, taxi!
   —Où allez-vous, madame?
   —Je vais à l'hôtel Méridien. #

Now check your answers. You should have matched the conversations with the places as follows: a-3, b-4, c-1, and d-2.

CD 9, Track 11

D. Questions et réponses, p. 124

Now it's your turn. Look at the pictures in your Workbook and say where each person is going.

Modèle: Est-ce qu'il va au restaurant ou au stade?
Il va au restaurant.

1. —Est-ce qu'elle va au supermarché ou à la bibliothèque? #
   —Elle va à la bibliothèque.

2. —Est-ce qu'il va au cinéma ou au supermarché? #
   —Il va au supermarché.

3. —Est-ce qu'ils vont à la plage ou à l'école? #
   —Ils vont à la plage.

4. —Est-ce qu'il va au garage ou à l'hôpital? #
   —Il va au garage.

CD 9, Track 12

E. Questions et réponses, p. 124

Listen to the questions and say that you are going to the places mentioned in your Workbook.

Modèle: Où vas-tu? #
Je vais au cinéma.

Commençons.

1. Où vas-tu? #   Je vais au supermarché.

2. Où vas-tu? #   Je vais à la piscine.

3. Où vas-tu? #   Je vais au café.

4. Où vas-tu? #   Je vais à la bibliothèque.

5. Où vas-tu? #   Je vais à l'école.

Section 3. Qu'est-ce que vous allez faire?

CD 9, Track 13

F. Compréhension orale, p. 125

Listen as someone asks people what they are going to do. In your Workbook, write the corresponding number next to the appropriate activity.

Modèle: 1. —Qu'est-ce que vous allez faire?
—Je vais jouer au tennis.

You would write the number "1" under picture "d" of the tennis scene.

2. —Qu'est-ce que vous allez faire?
   —Je vais faire une promenade. #

3. —Qu'est-ce que vous allez faire?
   —Nous allons jouer au volley. #

4. —Qu'est-ce que vous allez faire?
   —Je vais travailler. #

5. —Qu'est-ce que vous allez faire?
   —Nous allons nager.

6. —Qu'est-ce que vous allez faire?
   —Je vais téléphoner. #

Now the conversations are a bit longer. Again listen to find out what the people are going to do, and mark the activity in your Workbook.

7. —Où est-ce que tu vas?
   —Je vais au stade.
   —Et qu'est-ce que tu vas faire?
   —Ben . . . je vais jouer au foot. #

8. —Où est-ce que tu vas?
   —Dans ma chambre.
   —Qu'est-ce que tu vas faire?
   —Je vais regarder la télé. #

9. —Bonjour.
   —Bonjour.
   —Où est-ce que tu vas?
   —Je vais à la bibliothèque.
   —Qu'est-ce que tu vas faire?
   —Je vais étudier. Salut.
   —Salut. #

Now check your answers. You should have matched the conversations with the pictures as follows: a-5, b-2, c-4, d-1, e-6, f-3, g-8, h-9, and i-7.

CD 9, Track 14

G. Questions et réponses, p. 125

You will hear questions asking where you are going, followed by the name of an activity. Answer the question affirmatively saying you are going to do the activity mentioned.

Modèle: Tu vas au restaurant? # dîner #
            Oui, je vais dîner.

1. Tu vas à la piscine? # nager #
   Oui, je vais nager.

2. Tu vas à la bibliothèque? # étudier #
   Oui, je vais étudier.

3. Tu vas au stade? # jouer au foot #
   Oui, je vais jouer au foot.

4. Tu vas en ville? # faire une promenade #
   Oui, je vais faire une promenade.

5. Tu vas à une boum? # danser #
   Oui, je vais danser.

6. Tu vas chez un copain? # jouer aux jeux vidéo #
   Oui, je vais jouer aux jeux vidéo.

Section 4. Conversations

CD 9, Track 15

H. La réponse logique, p. 125

You will hear a series of short questions, each one read twice. In your Workbook, circle the letter (a, b, or c) corresponding to the most logical answer.

Commençons.

1. Où est-ce que tu dînes? #
2. Comment vas-tu en ville? #
3. Tu vas à la piscine? #
4. Qu'est-ce que tu fais samedi? #
5. Tu as un rendez-vous dimanche? #
6. Tu vas rester à la maison? #

Now check your answers. You should have circled 1-c, 2-a, 3-b, 4-a, 5-c, and 6-b.

Section 5. Dictée

CD 9, Track 16

I. Écoutez et écrivez., p. 126

You will hear a short dialogue spoken twice. First, listen carefully to what the people are saying. The second time you hear the dialogue, fill in the missing words.

Écoutez.
   —Vous restez à la maison aujourd'hui?
   —Non, nous allons en ville. Moi, je vais aller au cinéma.
   —Et ton frère?
   —Il a un rendez-vous avec une copine. Ils vont faire une promenade à pied dans le parc municipal.

Listen again and fill in the missing words.

BLEU

LESSON 14 QUIZ

Part I: Listening

CD 15, Track 2

A. Conversations

You will hear a series of short conversations between Christine and Jean-Paul. Listen to each conversation carefully. Then answer the corresponding questions on your answer sheet by circling the appropriate letter (a, b, or c). You will hear each conversation twice.

Let's begin.

1. JEAN-PAUL: Comment vas-tu à l'école?
   CHRISTINE: En général, je vais à pied.

2. CHRISTINE: Tu dînes au restaurant?
   JEAN-PAUL: Non, je dîne chez mon cousin.

3. JEAN-PAUL: Ta cousine est à la piscine?
   CHRISTINE: Non, elle est à la bibliothèque avec une copine.

4. JEAN-PAUL: Qu'est-ce que tu fais vendredi?
   CHRISTINE: J'ai rendez-vous avec Thomas.
   JEAN-PAUL: Où est-ce que vous allez?
   CHRISTINE: À un concert de rock.

5. CHRISTINE: Tu veux aller au cinéma avec moi?
   JEAN-PAUL: Non, je préfère rester à la maison.
   CHRISTINE: Ah bon, pourquoi?
   JEAN-PAUL: Je voudrais regarder un film à la télé.

6. JEAN-PAUL: Où vas-tu?
   CHRISTINE: Je vais à la plage.
   JEAN-PAUL: Tu vas nager?
   CHRISTINE: Non, je vais faire une promenade à pied.

Nom _____

Classe _____ Date _____ _____

Discovering FRENCH *Nouveau!*

B L E U

Unité 5
Leçon 14

Lesson Quiz

QUIZ 14

PART I: LISTENING

A. Conversations (30 points)

You will hear a series of short conversations between Christine and Jean-Paul. Listen to each conversation carefully. Then answer the corresponding questions on your answer sheet by circling the appropriate letter (a, b, or c). You will hear each conversation twice.

1. How does Christine get to school?
   a. She walks.
   b. She takes the bus.
   c. She rides her bicycle.

2. Where is Jean-Paul having dinner?
   a. At home.
   b. In a restaurant.
   c. At his cousin's house.

3. Where is Christine's cousin?
   a. At the swimming pool.
   b. At a friend's house.
   c. At the library.

4. What is Christine doing on Friday?
   a. She is going on a bicycle ride.
   b. She is going to a movie.
   c. She is going out with a friend.

5. What does Jean-Paul want to do?
   a. Study.
   b. Stay home.
   c. Go to a movie.

6. What is Christine going to do?
   a. Swim.
   b. Go for a walk.
   c. Play volleyball.

PART II: WRITING

B. Où sont-ils? (18 points)

Complete the following sentences with the appropriate form of **à** + DEFINITE ARTICLE.

1. Nous sommes _____ hôpital.

2. Tu nages _____ piscine.

3. Les élèves sont _____ musée.

4. Madame Lambert est _____ théâtre.

5. Les touristes restent _____ hôtel.

6. M. et Mme Chardon sont _____ Champs-Élysées.

Nom _____

Classe _____ Date _____

C. Qu'est-ce qu'ils vont faire? (24 points)

Describe what the following people are going to do, using the contraction **aller** + INFINITIVE.

1. Nous _____ .

2. Catherine et Valérie _____ .

3. Vous _____ un sandwich.

4. Tu _____ .

D. Expression personnelle (28 points)

For each of the times indicated below, mention one thing you are GOING TO DO and one thing you are NOT GOING TO DO.

• dimanche

[oui] _____

[non] _____

• pendant les vacances (*during vacation*)

[oui] _____

[non] _____

Nom _____

Classe _____ Date _____

Discovering
FRENCH
Nouveau!

BLEU

Unité 5
Leçon 15

Workbook TE

LEÇON 15 Au Café de l'Univers

LISTENING ACTIVITIES

Section 1. Je viens de . . .

A. Écoutez et répétez.

1. Je viens du café.
2. Tu viens du cinéma.
3. Elle vient de la plage.
4. Nous venons de la piscine.
5. Vous venez du supermarché.
6. Elles viennent du musée.

B. Questions et réponses

Modèle: —Tu vas au café?
            —**Non, je viens du café.**

1. Non, je viens du cinéma.
2. Non, je viens de la piscine.
3. Non, je viens du musée.
4. Non, je viens de la bibliothèque.
5. Non, je viens du restaurant.
6. Non, je viens de l'école.

Section 2. Les sports et la musique

C. Compréhension orale

a   b   c   d   e   f   g   h   i   j

D. Questions et réponses

▶ —Est-ce que Paul joue au tennis ou au ping-pong?
    —**Il joue au ping-pong.**

1. Il joue au tennis.   2. Il joue au basket.

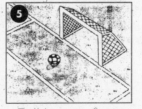

3. Elle joue au volley.   4. Il joue au baseball.   5. Il joue au foot.

Discovering French, Nouveau! Bleu

URB
p. 71

Unité 5, Leçon 15
Workbook

131

Nom _____

Classe _____ Date _____

Section 3. Les pronoms accentués

E. Écoutez et répétez.

Moi, je suis chez moi.

Toi, tu restes chez toi.

Lui, il étudie chez lui.

Elle, elle travaille chez elle.

Nous, nous dînons chez nous.

Vous, vous mangez chez vous.

Eux, ils regardent la télé chez eux.

Elles, elles mangent une pizza chez elles.

F. Parlez.

Modèle: Toi   **Tu vas chez toi.**
           Jean-Paul **Jean-Paul va chez lui.**

1. Stéphanie va chez elle.
2. Nicolas va chez lui.
3. Vous allez chez vous.
4. Nous allons chez nous.

5. Alice et Véronique vont chez elle.
6. Pierre et François vont chez eux.
7. Moi Je vais chez moi.
8. Mon cousin va chez lui.

Section 4. Conversations

G. La réponse logique

1. a. À pied.
    b. Au café.
    c. Du cinéma.

2. a. En ville.
    b. Du musée.
    c. À la bibliothèque.

3. a. J'ai une voiture de sport.
    b. Je joue aux cartes.
    c. C'est le foot.

4. a. Oui, j'aime la musique.
    b. Oui, je joue de la clarinette.
    c. Oui, je joue au baseball.

5. a. Non, mais je joue aux échecs.
    b. Oui, je joue du piano.
    c. Non, je n'aime pas la musique.

6. a. Oui, il est chez lui.
    b. Oui, il est chez moi.
    c. Oui, il est chez elle.

7. a. Oui, je vais chez moi.
    b. Oui, je suis chez moi.
    c. Oui, je vais chez un copain.

8. a. Oui, il aime le sport.
    b. Oui, il joue au foot.
    c. Oui, il a une Jaguar.

Section 5. Dictée

H. Écoutez et écrivez.

—Est-ce que ton copain est chez __lui__ ?

—Non, il __est__ __au__ cinéma avec son frère.

—À quelle heure est-ce qu'ils __reviennent__ __du__ cinéma?

—À six heures.

—Et qu'est-ce qu'ils vont __faire__ après *(afterwards)*?

—Ils rentrent *(are going back)* dîner chez __eux__ .

Nom _____

Classe _____ Date _____

Discovering FRENCH *Nouveau!*

B L E U

Unité 5
Leçon 15

Workbook TE

WRITING ACTIVITIES

A 1. La boum de Catherine

Catherine is organizing a party. Say who is coming and who is not, using the appropriate forms of **venir**.

▶ Claire a un examen demain.   Elle ne vient pas.

1. Philippe et Antoine aiment les boums.   Ils viennent.

2. Je dois étudier.   Je ne viens pas.

3. Nous aimons danser.   Nous venons.

4. Tu acceptes l'invitation.   Tu viens.

5. Vous n'êtes pas invités.   Vous ne venez pas.

6. Thomas est malade *(sick)*.   Il ne vient pas.

A/B 2. D'où viennent-ils?

It is dinner time and everyone is going home. Say which places each person is coming from.

▶ Éric vient du cinéma.

1.   2.   3.   4.   5.

1. Nathalie vient du supermarché .

2. Les élèves viennent de l'école .

3. Nous venons du café .

4. Monsieur Loiseau vient de la bibliothèque .

5. Vous venez du musée .

URB
Lp. 73

Discovering French, Nouveau! Bleu

Unité 5, Leçon 15
Workbook

133

Nom _____

Classe _____ Date _____

B 3. À la Maison des Jeunes

La Maison des Jeunes is a place where young people go for all kinds of different activities. Say what the following people are doing, using **jouer à** or **jouer de,** plus the illustrated activity.

▶ Nous jouons au ping-pong _____.

1. Diane joue de la guitare _____.

2. Stéphanie et Claire jouent au basket _____.

3. Vous jouez aux cartes _____.

4. Tu joues de la batterie _____.

5. Marc et Antoine jouent aux échecs _____.

6. Ma cousine joue du saxo(phone) _____.

C 4. Conversations

Complete the following mini-dialogues, using stress pronouns to replace the underlined nouns.

▶ —Tu dînes avec <u>Jean-Michel</u>?

—Oui, je dîne avec lui _____.

1. —Tu étudies avec <u>ta copine</u>?

—Oui, j'étudie avec elle _____.

2. —Tu travailles pour <u>Monsieur Moreau</u>?

—Oui, je travaille pour lui _____.

3. —Tu vas chez <u>Vincent et Thomas</u>?

—Oui, je vais chez eux _____.

4. —Tu voyages avec <u>Hélène et Alice</u>?

—Oui, je voyage avec elles _____.

URB
p. 74

134

Unité 5, Leçon 15
Workbook

Discovering French, Nouveau! Bleu

Nom _____

Classe _____ Date _____

5. L'orage *(The storm)*

Because of the storm, everyone is staying home today. Express this by completing the sentences below with **chez** and the appropriate stress pronoun.

▶ Nous étudions *chez nous* _____.

1. Monsieur Beaumont reste *chez lui* _____.

2. Madame Vasseur travaille *chez elle* _____.

3. Je regarde un DVD *chez moi* _____.

4. Tu joues aux jeux vidéo *chez toi* _____.

5. Vous dînez *chez vous* _____.

6. Vincent et Philippe jouent aux échecs *chez eux* _____.

7. Cécile et Sophie étudient *chez elles* _____.

8. Jean-Paul regarde la télé *chez lui* _____.

D 6. Qu'est-ce que c'est?

Identify the following objects more specifically.

▶ C'est une raquette *de tennis* _____.

1. C'est une raquette *de ping-pong* _____. 4. C'est un album *de photos* _____.

2. C'est un ballon *de foot* _____. 5. C'est un livre *d'espagnol* _____.

3. C'est une batte *de baseball* _____. 6. C'est un CD *de jazz* _____.

Nom _____

Classe _____ Date _____

7.  Communication (sample answers)

1. **Et vous?**
   Describe your leisure activities.
   Say . . .

   - *which sports you play*   Je joue au foot et au basket.
   - *which games you play*   Je joue aux jeux d'ordinateur.
   - *which instrument(s) you play*   Je joue de la flûte et du piano.

2. **Lettre à Jérôme**
   Your friend Jérôme is going to spend Saturday with you.
   Ask him . . .

   - *at what time he is coming*
   - *if he plays tennis*
   - *if he has a tennis racket*
   - *if he likes to play chess*

   Tell him that you are going to have dinner at your cousins'.

   Ask him . . .

   - *if he wants to go to their place too*
   - *what time he has to go home*

   > À quelle heure viens-tu (est-ce que tu viens)?
   > Est-ce que tu joues au tennis?
   > Est-ce que tu as une raquette de tennis?
   > Est-ce que tu aimes jouer aux échecs?
   > Je vais dîner chez mes cousin(e)s.
   >
   > Est-ce que tu veux aller chez eux (elles) aussi?
   >
   > À quelle heure est-ce que tu dois rentrer chez toi?

LEÇON 15   Au Café de l'Univers

A

Activité 1   Venir ou revenir

Circle the correct form of the verb to complete each sentence.

1. —Nous (venons)/ venez chez toi à huit heures. D'accord?
   —D'accord!

2. —D'où revenons / (revenez) vous?
   —De la bibliothèque.

3. —Est-ce que tu (viens)/ venez au café avec nous?
   —Non, je ne peux pas, j'ai un examen demain.

4. —Maman, je vais chez ma copine. Je (reviens)/ revient à 6 heures.
   —Bon, vas-y. À ce soir!

Activité 2   Prépositions

Fill in the blanks with **de, du, de la, de l',** or **des** to complete these sentences.

1. Nicole est ___de___ Nice.

2. La bibliothèque ___de l'___ école est assez petite.

3. Ce sont les livres ___des___ profs.

4. Est-ce que le frère ___d'___ Éric est sympathique?

5. ___De___ qui est-ce que tu parles?

6. Est-ce que tu joues ___du___ violon ou ___de la___ guitare?

Activité 3   Dialogues

Making your selections from the box, fill in the blanks with stress pronouns.

—Ce soir, tu vas chez Gisèle?
—Oui, je vais chez ___elle___.
—Je peux venir avec toi?
—Mais oui, tu peux venir avec ___moi___!
—Et demain, tu vas au musée avec tes parents?
—Oui, et je vais aussi au restaurant avec ___eux___.

—Tu viens en voiture avec Cédric?
—Oui, je viens avec ___lui___.
—Vous mangez chez vous ce soir?
—Oui, nous mangeons chez ___nous___.

moi
toi
lui
elle
nous
vous
eux
elles

Nom _____

Classe _____ Date _____

Discovering
FRENCH
Nouveau!

B L E U

B

Activité 1   Dialogues

First, circle the correct verb form in each question. Then, match each question with its most logical response.

_c_ 1. —Qui *vient* / *venez* chez moi?

_e_ 2. —Est-ce que Pierre *reviens* / *revient* de la bibliothèque?

_a_ 3. —Est-ce qu'elles *viennent* / *vient* de Nice?

_b_ 4. —D'où *viens-tu* / *venez-tu*?

_d_ 5. —Est-ce que vous *revenez* / *revenons* de la piscine?

a. —Oui, elles sont françaises.

b. —Je viens de Québec.

c. —Moi, je viens chez toi!

d. —Oui, nous nageons beaucoup.

e. —Oui, il a des livres.

Activité 2   Prépositions

Fill in the blanks with **de, de la, de l', d'** or **des** to complete the sentences.

1. Mon frère aime les jeux _d'_____ ordinateur, mais je préfère jouer _de la_____ guitare.

2. —Je viens _de_____ Strasbourg. Et toi? —Je viens _d'_____ Annecy.

3. Monique joue _de la_____ batterie dans un groupe _de_____ musique rock.

4. Inès parle _de_____ ses problèmes avec sa copine Patricia.

Activité 3   Une conversation au téléphone

Fill in the blanks to complete a conversation between Karine and her friend Nicole, making your selections from the box.

moi	toi	lui	elle	nous	vous	qui

Allô, Karine?

Oui. C'est _toi_____, Nicole?

Oui, c'est _moi_____!

Tu veux venir à une boum, samedi?

C'est chez _qui_____?

Chez Marco.

Chez _lui_____?
Mais sa maman est d'accord?

Mais oui!

OK, c'est super. Maman demande si tu déjeunes ici chez _nous_____.

Merci, je veux bien!

Nom _____

Classe _____ Date _____ _____

Discovering
FRENCH *Nouveau!*

B L E U

Unité 5
Leçon 15
Activités pour tous TE

C

Activité 1 À quelle heure?

The party is at 8:00 but some people are coming a little earlier or later. Write sentences that say when each person is coming.

Modèle: Je viens à 8h30.

1. Tu / 7h30 Tu viens à 7h30.
2. Caroline / 8h Caroline vient à 8h.
3. Vous / 7h45 Vous venez à 7h45.
4. Bernard et Patrick / 8h15 Bernard et Patrick viennent à 8h15.
5. Anne et moi / 8h30 Anne et moi venons à 8h30.

Activité 2 L'orchestre

Your pen pal is telling you about his school orchestra. Fill in the blanks with **de.**

Je joue dans l'orchestre de l' école. C'est un petit orchestre:

il y a six membres. Nous jouons de la musique classique,

du jazz et de la musique internationale. Trinh

joue du piano, Ariane et Guy jouent du

violon, et moi, je joue de la flûte. Julianne et Frédéric ont beaucoup

de talent. Elle joue de la guitare classique et du

violon. Il joue de la batterie, du saxophone

et de la flûte! Et toi, est-ce que tu joues d'un instrument

de musique?

Activité 3 Tu es sûr?

Your friend is having a hard time deciphering who is in some of the pictures you are showing her. Clarify it for her by using stress pronouns.

1. —Qui est-ce? Est-ce que c'est Marc?
   —Oui, c'est lui .

2. —Qui est-ce? C'est Bruno et toi?
   —Oui, c'est nous .

3. —Qui est-ce? Est-ce que ce sont tes parents?
   —Oui, c'est eux .

4. —Qui est-ce? Est-ce que ce sont tes petites soeurs?
   —Oui, c'est elles .

5. —Qui est-ce? Est-ce que c'est Virginie?
   —Oui, c'est elle .

6. —Ce n'est pas vrai! C'est moi?
   —Mais oui, c'est toi !

LEÇON 15 Au Café de l'Univers, page 216

Objectives

Communicative Functions and Topics	To talk about activities: sports, games, and music
	To talk about where people are coming from
	To contradict someone
	To express surprise
Linguistic Goals	To use stress pronouns and contractions with *de*
	To use the verb *venir*
	To use the construction noun + *de* + noun
	To pronounce vowels /ø/ and /œ/
Cultural Goals	To learn about attractions in Paris and in French cafés

Motivation and Focus

❏ Look at the photos on pages 216–217 and ask the class to imagine they are in the café with friends. What might they talk about? Brainstorm a list of topics.

Presentation and Explanation

❏ *Lesson Opener:* Follow the SETTING THE STAGE suggestions on page 216 of the TE, listing conversation topics on the board. After listening to **Audio CD** 3, Tracks 9–10, or your reading of the opening text, have students read it and discuss what topics the girls talk about. Make comparisons between the topics students listed and those in the monologue.

❏ *Note culturelle:* Have students read *Au café*, page 217. Encourage them to compare activities in French cafés to their own favorite gathering places.

❏ *Grammar A and B:* Introduce the verb *venir* and the preposition *de,* pages 218–219. Model and have students repeat the forms and examples.

❏ *Vocabulaire:* Present vocabulary for sports, games, and music using the box on page 220. Have students repeat the words and actions. Model the verbs used to talk about sports and music. Encourage students to talk about the sports and musical instruments they play.

❏ *Grammar C:* Introduce stress pronouns, page 221, by following the TEACHING STRATEGY idea in the TE margin. Use **Overhead Transparency** 16.

❏ *Vocabulary:* Call attention to the expressions for contradicting someone and for expressing surprise, page 222. Encourage students to copy intonation and facial expressions as they practice these phrases.

❏ *Grammar D:* As you present the construction noun + *de* + noun, page 223, use the CRITICAL THINKING suggestion in the TE margin to help students draw conclusions about French word order.

❏ *Prononciation:* Use **Audio CD** 3, Track 11 or model the text in the box, page 223, to focus students' attention on the vowel sounds /ø/ and /œ/. Have students repeat the words.

Guided Practice and Checking Understanding

❏ Play **Audio CD** 9, Tracks 17–24 or read the **Audioscript** to check listening comprehension with **Workbook** Listening Activities A–H, pages 131–132.

❏ Use the **Video** or **Videoscript** as students do **Video Activities** pages 91–93.

Independent Practice

❏ Practice vocabulary and structures with the activities on pages 218–223. Students can do Activities 2, 3, and 7 for homework. Arrange students in pairs to check their answers

together. Model and have students repeat the exchanges in Activities 1, 4–6, 8, and 9. Students can then do the activities as PAIR PRACTICE, switching roles to allow for more practice.

❑ Use **Communipak** *Tête à tête* 3, pages 157–158, and *Échanges* 3–4, pages 151–152, for pair practice in asking and answering questions about sports, music, and games. **Video Activities** page 94 can be done in small groups.

❑ Have students do the activities in **Activités pour tous,** pages 79–81.

Monitoring and Adjusting

❑ Assign **Workbook** Writing Activities 1–7 on pages 133–136.

❑ Monitor students' language as they work on the activities. Explain the grammar and vocabulary boxes as needed. Use the TOURING PARIS activity, pages 218–219 of the TE, to monitor use of *aller . . . à, venir . . . de,* and contractions.

Assessment

❑ Administer Quiz 15 on pages 101–102 after the lesson's activities are completed. Adapt the test items to your class's needs using the **Test Generator**.

Reteaching

❑ Redo any appropriate activities in the **Workbook**.

❑ Use the **Video** to reteach portions of the lesson.

Extension and Enrichment

❑ Students can do CHALLENGE, page 225 of the TE, to prepare their own illustrated messages. Expand the conversational practice of inviting friends to come along and identifying people by using CHALLENGE, page 218 of the TE. Introduce names of additional sports and musical instruments in SUPPLEMENTARY VOCABULARY, page 220 of the TE.

Summary and Closure

❑ Replay the **Video** for the lesson or have students look back through the lesson in the textbook. Students can work in cooperative groups to make a list of Paris attractions. Encourage students to talk about what places they would like to go to and explain why.

❑ Do PORTFOLIO ASSESSMENT on page 225 of the TE.

End-of-Lesson Activities

❑ *À votre tour!:* Students can prepare and practice Activities 1–3 on page 224. Use **Audio CD 3,** Tracks 12–13 with Activities 1–2. Assign Activities 4 and 5 on page 225 for written homework. Follow the suggestions at the bottom of page 224 of the TE for PAIR PRACTICE.

LEÇON 15 Au Café de l'Univers, page 216

Block Scheduling (3 days to complete)

Objectives

Communicative Functions and Topics
To talk about activities: sports, games, and music
To talk about where people are coming from
To contradict someone
To express surprise

Linguistic Goals
To use stress pronouns and contractions with *de*
To use the verb *venir*
To use the construction noun + *de* + noun
To pronounce vowels /ø/ and /œ/

Cultural Goals
To learn about attractions in Paris and in French cafés

Day 1

Motivation and Focus

❑ Look at the photos on pages 216–217 and ask the class to imagine they are in the café with friends. What might they talk about? Brainstorm a list of topics.

Presentation and Explanation

❑ *Lesson Opener:* Follow the SETTING THE STAGE suggestions on page 216 of the TE, listing conversation topics on the board. After listening to **Audio CD** 3, Tracks 9–10, or your reading of the opening text, have students read it and discuss what topics the girls talk about. Make comparisons between the topics students listed and those in the monologue.

❑ *Note culturelle:* Have students read *Au café*, page 217. Encourage them to compare activities in French cafés to their own favorite gathering places.

❑ *Grammar A and B:* Introduce the verb *venir* and the preposition *de*, pages 218–219. Model and have students repeat the forms and examples.

❑ *Vocabulaire:* Present vocabulary for sports, games, and music using the box on page 220. Have students repeat the words and actions. Model the verbs used to talk about sports and music. Encourage students to talk about the sports and musical instruments they play.

❑ *Grammar C:* Introduce stress pronouns, page 221, by following the TEACHING STRATEGY idea in the TE margin. Use **Overhead Transparency** 16.

❑ *Vocabulary:* Call attention to the expressions for contradicting someone and for expressing surprise, page 222. Encourage students to copy intonation and facial expressions as they practice these phrases.

❑ *Grammar D:* As you present the construction noun + *de* + noun, page 223, use the CRITICAL THINKING suggestion in the TE margin to help students draw conclusions about French word order.

❑ *Prononciation:* Use **Audio CD** 3, Track 11 or model the text in the box, page 223, to focus students' attention on the vowel sounds /ø/ and /œ/. Have students repeat the words.

Guided Practice and Checking Understanding

❑ Play **Audio CD** 9, Tracks 17–24 or read the **Audioscript** to check listening comprehension with **Workbook** Listening Activities A–H, pages 131–132.

Day 2

Motivation and Focus

❑ Use the **Video** or **Videoscript** as students do **Video Activities** pages 91–93.

Independent Practice

❑ Practice vocabulary and structures with the activities on pages 218–223. Students can do Activities 2, 3 and 7 for homework. Arrange students in pairs to check their answers. Model and have students repeat the exchanges in Activities 1, 4–6, 8, and 9.

❑ Use **Communipak** *Tête à tête* 3, pages 157–158 and *Échanges* 3-4, pages 151–152, for pair practice in asking and answering questions about sports, music, and games.

❑ Have students do the activities in **Activités pour tous,** pages 79–81.

Monitoring and Adjusting

❑ Assign **Workbook** Writing Activities 1–7 on pages 133–136.

❑ Explain the grammar and vocabulary boxes as needed. Use the TOURING PARIS Activity, pages 218–219 of the TE, to monitor use of *aller . . . à, venir . . . de*, and contractions.

Day 3

End-of-Lesson Activities

❑ *À votre tour!:* Students can do Activities 1–3 on page 224. Use **Audio** CD 3, Tracks 12–13 with Activities 1–2. Assign 4 and 5 on page 225 for homework. Follow the suggestions at the bottom of page 224 of the TE for PAIR PRACTICE.

❑ Use **Block Scheduling Copymasters,** pages 113–120.

Reteaching (as needed)

❑ Redo activities in the **Workbook** and use the **Video** to reteach parts of the lesson.

Extension and Enrichment (as desired)

❑ Students can do CHALLENGE, page 225 of the TE, to prepare their own illustrated messages. Expand the conversational practice of inviting friends to come along and identifying people by using CHALLENGE, page 218 of the TE. Introduce names of additional sports and musical instruments in SUPPLEMENTARY VOCABULARY, page 220 of the TE.

❑ For expansion activities, direct students to www.classzone.com.

Summary and Closure

❑ Do PORTFOLIO ASSESSMENT on page 225 of the TE.

Assessment

❑ Administer Quiz 15 on pages 101–102 after the lesson's activities are completed. Adapt the test items to students' needs using the **Test Generator**.

Nom _____

Classe _____ Date _____

Discovering
FRENCH
Nouveau!

BLEU

LEÇON 15 Au Café de l'Univers, pages 216–217

Materials Checklist

- **Student Text**
- **Audio CD** 3, Tracks 9–10
- **Video** 3 or **DVD** 2; Counter 15:43–20:23

Steps to Follow

- Before you read the passage on p. 216, read the *Compréhension* questions on p. 217. They will help you understand the passage and the audio or video.
- Read the passage on p. 216 before you listen to the audio or watch the video.
- Watch **Video** 3 or **DVD** 2; Counter 15:43–20:23, or listen to **Audio CD** 3, Tracks 9–10.
- Answer the *Compréhension* questions (p. 217) on a separate sheet of paper.
- Write the answers to *Et toi?* (p. 217).
- Read the *Note culturelle* (p. 217); write any expressions you do not understand on a separate sheet of paper. Check meanings.

If You Don't Understand . . .

- Watch the **Video** or **DVD** in a quiet place. Try to stay focused. If you get lost, stop the **Video** or **DVD**. Replay it and find your place.
- Listen to the **CD** in a quiet place. Try to stay focused. If you get lost, stop the **CD**. Replay it and find your place.
- Repeat aloud with the audio. Try to sound like the people on the recording.
- On a separate sheet of paper, write down the words that are underlined in the text. Check for meaning.
- Say aloud anything you write. Make sure you understand everything you say.
- Write down any questions so that you can ask your partner or your teacher later.

Self-Check

Answer the following true/false questions on a separate sheet of paper.

1. On ne peut pas manger un sandwich dans un café français.
2. Les jeunes Français vont au café principalement pour étudier.
3. Dans les cybercafés on peut surfer sur l'Internet.
4. Un café français est divisé en deux parties.
5. Au printemps et en été les Français préfèrent s'asseoir à l'intérieur.

Answers

1. False 2. False 3. True 4. True 5. False

Nom _____

Classe _____ Date _____

Discovering
FRENCH *Nouveau!*

B L E U

Unité 5
Leçon 15
Absent Student Copymasters

A. Le verbe *venir,* page 218

Materials Checklist

- **Student Text**
- **Audio CD** 9, Track 17
- **Workbook**

Steps to Follow

- Study *Le verbe venir* (p. 218). Copy the conjugation and read it aloud.
- Study the different meanings of **venir** and **revenir** (p. 218). Write the conjugation of **revenir**.
- Do Activity 1 in the text (p. 218). Write the parts for both speakers. Underline the present tense forms of **venir**. Read both parts aloud.
- Do Activity 2 in the text (p. 218). Write your answers in complete sentences on a separate sheet of paper. Underline the different forms of **venir**.
- Do **Writing Activities** A 1 in the **Workbook** (p. 133).
- Do **Listening Activities** A in the **Workbook** (p. 131). Use **Audio CD** 9, Track 17.

If You Don't Understand . . .

- Listen to the **CD** in a quiet place. Try to stay focused. If you get lost, stop the **CD**. Replay it and find your place.
- Reread the activity directions. Put the directions in your own words.
- Say aloud everything that you write. Be sure you understand what you are saying.
- Write down questions so that you can ask your partner or your teacher later.
- When writing a sentence, ask yourself, "What do I mean? What am I trying to say?"

Self-Check

On a separate sheet of paper, say who is coming to the party. Use the appropriate pronoun, and write complete sentences.

1. Anne (oui)
2. Thomas et Annette (non)
3. Tu (oui)
4. Nous (oui)
5. Vous (non)
6. Jeanne et Alice (non)
7. Je (oui)

Answers

7. Je viens à la boum.
venons à la boum. 5. Vous ne venez pas à la boum. 6. Elles ne viennent pas à la boum.
1. Elle vient à la boum. 2. Ils ne viennent pas à la boum. 3. Tu viens à la boum. 4. Nous

Unité 5
Leçon 15

Absent Student
Copymasters

Discovering
FRENCH
Nouveau!

BLEU

Nom _____

Classe _____ Date _____

B. La préposition *de*; *de* + l'article défini, pages 219–220

Materials Checklist

- **Student Text**
- **Audio CD** 9, Tracks 18–20
- **Video** 3 or **DVD** 2; Counter 14:20–20:23
- **Workbook**

Steps to Follow

- Study *La préposition **de**; **de** + l'article défini* (p. 219).
- Write the singular and plural forms of **de** and the definite article. Underline the contractions.
- Watch **Video** 3 or **DVD** 2; Counter 14:20–20:23.
- Do Activity 3 in the text (p. 219). Write the answers on a separate sheet. Read them aloud. Underline contractions, for example, **Isabelle vient du parc de la Villette.**
- Do Activity 4 in the text (p. 220). Write the answers on a separate sheet of paper. Read them aloud. Underline the contractions, for example, **Je viens du café.**
- Study *Vocabulaire: Les sports, les jeux et la musique* (p. 220). Write the vocabulary on a separate sheet of paper. Check meanings.
- Do Activity 5 in the text (p. 220). Answer the questions in complete sentences.
- Do **Writing Activities** A/B 2 and B 3 in the **Workbook** (pp. 133–134).
- Do **Listening Activities** B–D in the **Workbook** (p. 131). Use **Audio CD** 9, Tracks 18–20.

If You Don't Understand . . .

- Watch the **Video** or **DVD** in a quiet place. Try to stay focused. If you get lost, stop the **Video** or **DVD**. Replay it and find your place.
- Listen to the **CD** in a quiet place. Try to stay focused. If you get lost, stop the **CD**. Replay it and find your place.
- Reread the activity directions. Put the directions in your own words.
- Read the model several times. Be sure you understand it.
- Write down questions so that you can ask your partner or your teacher later.

Self-Check

Answer the following questions on a separate sheet of paper. Use the appropriate pronoun, and write complete sentences.

1. D'où vient Sylvie? (le restaurant)
2. D'où viennent Hélène et Anne? (la piscine)
3. D'où viens-tu? (la bibliothèque)
4. Qu'est-ce que vous jouez? (la guitare)

Answers

1. Elle vient du restaurant. 2. Elles viennent de la piscine. 3. Je viens de la bibliothèque. 4. Je joue de la guitare. / Nous jouons de la guitare.

Nom _____

Classe _____ Date _____

Discovering
FRENCH *Nouveau!*
BLEU

Unité 5
Leçon 15
Absent Student
Copymasters

C. Les pronoms accentués, pages 221–222

Materials Checklist

- **Student Text**
- **Audio CD** 9, Tracks 21–22
- **Workbook**

Steps to Follow

- Study *Les pronoms accentués* Forms (p. 221). Say the model sentences aloud. Copy the models on a separate sheet of paper.
- Study *Les pronoms accentués* Uses (p. 221). Say the model sentences aloud. Copy the models.
- Do Activities 6 and 7 in the text (p. 222). Write the answers in complete sentences on a separate sheet of paper.
- Study *Vocabulaire: Expressions pour la conversation* (p. 222).
- Do Activity 8 in the text (p. 222). Write out the dialogues in complete sentences. Read them aloud.
- Do **Writing Activities** C 4, 5 in the **Workbook** (pp. 134–135).
- Do **Listening Activities** E–F in the **Workbook** (p. 132). Use **Audio CD** 9, Tracks 21–22.

If You Don't Understand . . .

- Listen to the **CD** in a quiet place. Try to stay focused. If you get lost, stop the **CD**. Replay it and find your place.
- Reread the activity directions. Put the directions in your own words.
- Read the model several times before beginning so you are certain what to do. Copy the model. Underline the stress pronouns, for example, **Oui, il dîne avec <u>elle</u>.**
- Say aloud everything that you write. Listen and be sure you understand what you are saying.
- Write down any questions so that you can ask your teacher or your partner later.

Self-Check

Replace the underlined word or words in each sentence with the appropriate stress pronoun.

1. Alain dîne avec <u>Jean</u>.
2. Alice va chez <u>Marie</u>.
3. Nous jouons au basket avec <u>Paul et Anne</u>.
4. Tu fais une promenade avec <u>moi et mon ami</u>.
5. Philippe travaille avec <u>Hélène et Louise</u>.
6. Jeanne et Marie restent à la maison avec <u>toi et ta soeur</u>.

Answers

1. lui 2. elle 3. eux 4. nous 5. elles 6. vous

Nom _____

Classe _____ Date _____

Discovering
FRENCH
Nouveau!

BLEU

D. La construction nom + *de* + nom, page 223

Materials Checklist

- **Student Text**
- **Audio CD** 3, Tracks 11–13; **CD** 9, Tracks 23–24
- **Workbook**

Steps to Follow

- Study *La construction: nom + **de** + nom* (p. 223). Say the model sentences aloud. Copy the models on a separate sheet of paper.
- Do Activity 9 in the text (p. 223). Write the answers in complete sentences on a separate sheet of paper.
- Read the list of words in *Prononciation: Les voyelles /ø/ and /œ/* (p. 223). Listen to *Prononciation: Les voyelles /ø/ and /œ/* on **Audio** CD 3, Track 11. Repeat what you hear.
- Do **Writing Activities** D 6, 7 in the **Workbook** (pp. 135–136).
- Do **Listening Activities** G–H in the **Workbook** (p. 132). Use **Audio CD** 9, Tracks 23–24.
- Do Activities 1–5 of *À votre tour!* in the text (pp. 224–225). Use **Audio CD** 3, Tracks 12–13 with Activities 1 and 2.

If You Don't Understand . . .

- Reread the activity directions. Put the directions in your own words.
- Read the model several times before beginning so you are certain what to do. Copy the model. Underline the expressions with noun + **de** + noun, for example, **C'est une raquette de tennis.**
- Say aloud everything that you write. Listen and be sure you understand what you are saying.
- Write down any questions so that you can ask your teacher or your partner later.
- Listen to the **CDs** in a quiet place. Try to stay focused. If you get lost, stop the **CDs**. Replay them and find your place.
- Repeat aloud with the audio. Try to sound like the people on the recording. Imitate their sounds and accents. Pause the **CD** if you need to.

Self-Check

Use the following expressions to tell what each person has. Write complete sentences on a separate sheet of paper.

1. Jean / voiture / sport
2. Alice / raquette / tennis
3. Nous / livre / anglais
4. Vous / album / photos
5. Tu / leçon / flute
6. Jeanne et Marie / CD / la musique classique

Answers

Nom _____

Classe _____ Date _____

Discovering
FRENCH *Nouveau!*

B L E U

Unité 5
Leçon 15

Leçon 15

Family Involvement

LEÇON 15 Au café de l'Univers

Les sports

Ask a family member which sport he or she wants to play.

- First, explain your assignment.
- Model the pronunciation of the words under each picture. Point to the picture as you model each answer.
- Ask the question: **À quel sport veux-tu jouer?**
- After you get the answer, complete the sentence at the bottom of the page.

le tennis

le volleyball

le baseball

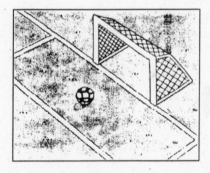

le football

_____ veut jouer au _____.

Nom _____

Classe _____ Date _____

La musique

Find out what musical instrument a family member likes.

- First, explain your assignment.
- Model the pronunciation of each word below the pictures. Point to the picture as you model each answer.
- Ask the question: **Quel instrument est-ce que tu aimes?**
- When you have an answer, complete the sentence at the bottom of the page.

la guitare

la clarinette

le piano

le violon

la flûte

la batterie

_____ aime _____.

Nom _____

Classe _____ Date _____

Discovering
FRENCH
Nouveau!

BLEU

Unité 5
Leçon 15

Video Activities

MODULE 15 Sports et musique

Video 3, DVD 2

15.1 Activité 1. Quels sports est-ce que vous pratiquez?   Counter 15:43–16:11

French teenagers participate in many different sports. What sports do the five teenagers in the video tell us they play? Number the names of sports below in the order you hear them in the video. You will hear two of the sports mentioned twice.

a. _____ tennis   c. _____ foot   e. _____ ping-pong

b. _____ basket   d. _____ volley

15.2 Activité 2. Sorties *(Outings)*   Counter 16:12–16:32

What are people doing and where are they going? As you watch the video segment, circle the letter of the appropriate completion to each sentence below. The sentences are given in the order you hear them in the video.

1. **Nous allons . . .**

   a. au parc
   b. au gymnase
   c. à la piscine

2. **Vous allez jouer au . . . ?**

   a. tennis
   b. basket
   c. volley

3. **Nous allons faire . . .**

   a. un voyage
   b. un match
   c. une promenade

4. **Tu joues au . . . ?**

   a. baseball
   b. ping-pong
   c. football

5. **Tu veux jouer . . . ?**

   a. avec moi
   b. avec lui
   c. avec elle

URB
p. 91

Nom _____

Classe _____ Date _____

15.3 Activité 3. Est-ce que Paul joue au tennis?

Counter 16:33–17:21

What sports are people playing? After you watch the video segment, draw a line from each sentence to the corresponding picture.

a.

b.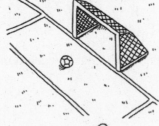

c.

1. Il joue au ping-pong.

2. Il joue au tennis.

3. Elle joue au basket.

4. Elle joue au volley.

5. Il joue au baseball.

6. Il joue au foot.

d.

e.

f.

15.4 Activité 4. Au conservatoire

Counter 17:22–18:20

What instruments do students at the **conservatoire** play? As you watch the video, mark an **X** next to the name of each instrument below you hear mentioned.

a. _____ la guitare   f. _____ le violon

b. _____ la flûte   g. _____ la batterie

c. _____ le trombone   h. _____ la clarinette

d. _____ le saxo   i. _____ la trompette

e. _____ le piano

Nom _____

Classe _____ Date _____

Discovering
FRENCH
Nouveau!

B L E U

Unité 5
Leçon 15
Video Activities

15.5 Activité 5. Interview avec Éric   Counter 18:21–18:55

Watch the interview with Éric and circle the letter of the correct completion to the statements below.

1. Éric adore . . .   a. la musique   b. les instruments

2. Il préfère . . .   a. le rock et le jazz   b. la musique classique

3. Il joue . . .   a. du piano   b. de la batterie

4. Il joue . . .   a. chez lui   b. dans un orchestre

5. Il joue dans les boums le . . .   a. vendredi   b. samedi

15.6 Activité 6. À la Maison des Jeunes   Counter 18:56–20:23

A. Before you watch the **Vignette culturelle,** answer the following question.

Question personnelle: Where do you go to do activities like sports, games, and hobbies?

Réponse: _____

B. Now, as you watch the **Vignette culturelle**, answer the questions below.

1. What is **la Maison des Jeunes et de la Culture?** _____

2. What do French teenagers do there? _____

_____

C. Question personnelle: Would you like to go to a **Maison des Jeunes?** If so, what would you do there?

Réponse: _____

Nom _____

Classe _____ Date _____

  Activité 7. Un jeu: Activités

Imagine you are at a **Maison des Jeunes** with your friends. In teams of four or five students, say what activities you do there. To start, the first student says a sentence using illustration 1. The second student says a sentence using illustration 2 and adds the first student's activity. Then the third student continues. If a student makes a mistake, *he or she must start over from the beginning.* The winning team is the first group that incorporates all the activities into the list without making any mistakes. Remember to use **jouer à** or **jouer de** as appropriate.

▶   ÉLÈVE 1:   **À la Maison des Jeunes, je joue de la guitare.**
    ÉLÈVE 2:   **À la Maison des Jeunes, je joue de la clarinette et de la guitare.**
    ÉLÈVE 3:   **À la Maison des Jeunes, je joue au basket. Je joue aussi de la clarinette et de la guitare.**

Discovering
FRENCH
Nouveau!

BLEU

Unité 5
Leçon 15

Videoscripts

MODULE 15 Sports et musique

Video 3, DVD 2

French teenagers love sports. They play tennis, volleyball, and basketball. They may swim at the local pool or at the beach. At school, they play all types of sports. But the sport they play most often is soccer. There are town and school teams. And on weekends, teams play for the local championship.

French people love to watch their favorite teams play for the national championship which is known as «Le Championnat de France». To encourage their teams, fans fill the stadiums, such as the Stade de France near Paris which holds 80,000 spectators.

French soccer players are among the best in the world. In 1998, the French national team, recognizable by its blue jerseys and known as les Bleus, won the World Cup by beating the favorite team, Brazil, by a score of 3 to 0. The leading player, Zinedine Zidane, a Frenchman of Algerian origin, instantly became a national hero.

15.1 Mini-scenes: Listening—Quels sports est-ce que vous pratiquez?
Counter 15:43–16:11

Let's ask some French teenagers which sports they participate in. **Quels sports est-ce que vous pratiquez?**

—Je joue au ping-pong.
—Je joue au tennis.
—Je joue au basket.
—Je joue au foot.
—Je joue au volley.
—Et moi, je joue au foot … et au tennis aussi.

15.2 Mini-scenes: Listening— Tu veux jouer au volley?
Counter 16:12–16:32

Now watch the following conversations. Can you understand which sports the students are talking about?

—Où allez-vous?
—Nous allons au gymnase.
—Vous allez jouer au basket?
—Oui, nous allons faire un match.

—Tu joues au ping-pong?
—Oui.
—Tu joues bien?
—Assez bien.
—Tu veux jouer avec moi?
—D'accord.

15.3 Mini-scenes: Speaking— Est-ce que Paul joue au tennis?
Counter 16:33–17:21

Now it's your turn. Answer the questions, saying that the people are participating in the sport shown on the screen. Follow the model.

—Est-ce que Paul joue au tennis ou au ping-pong?
—Il joue au ping-pong.

—Est-ce qu'il joue au volley ou au tennis?
[Il joue au tennis.]

—Est-ce qu'elle joue au volley ou au basket?
[Elle joue au basket.]

—Est-ce qu'elle joue au volley ou au foot?
[Elle joue au volley.]

—Est-ce qu'il joue au foot ou au baseball?
[Il joue au baseball.]

—Est-ce qu'il joue au foot ou au basket?
[Il joue au foot.]

15.4 Mini-scenes: Listening—De quel instrument est-ce que tu joues?
Counter 17:22–18:20

French teenagers also love music. They listen to their favorite CDs on their portable players or their home stereos. On weekends, many young people go to

concerts. *Many also play a musical instrument. Some take lessons at* **le conservatoire** *or music school.*

Let's go to **le Conservatoire municipal Claude Debussy** *and ask students what instruments they play.*

De quel instrument est-ce que tu joues?

—Je joue de la flûte.
—Je joue du piano.
—Je joue du saxo.
—Je joue de la clarinette.
—Je joue de la guitare.
—Je joue de la batterie.
—Je joue du violon.

15.5 Dialogue: Interview avec Éric

Counter 18:21–18:55

ISABELLE: Now we're going to meet Éric, who plays in a small band.
Tu aimes la musique?

ÉRIC: J'adore ça.

ISABELLE: Quel type de musique est-ce que tu préfères?

ÉRIC: J'aime le rock et le jazz.

ISABELLE: Tu joues d'un instrument?

ÉRIC: Ben oui … je joue de la batterie.

ISABELLE: Tu joues souvent?

ÉRIC: Oui, assez souvent. Je joue dans un orchestre avec des copains.

ISABELLE: Quand est-ce que vous jouez?

ÉRIC: Le samedi, dans des boums. C'est super. On s'amuse et on gagne de l'argent.

ISABELLE: Merci. Au revoir!

ÉRIC: Au revoir.

15.6 Vignette culturelle: À la Maison des Jeunes

Counter 18:56–20:23

Most French cities have **une Maison des Jeunes et de la Culture***. Let's visit* **La Maison des Jeunes de Créteil***, a suburb of Paris.*

Do you like to play tennis? ping-pong? Do you play a musical instrument? Or are you interested in dance? or in arts and crafts? French teenagers who enjoy these activities can go to their local **Maison des Jeunes***.*

Now let's talk to some young people.

—Qu'est-ce que tu aimes faire ici?
—J'aime bien faire de la danse, parce qu'on est en groupe et je suis avec mes amis.
—Et toi?
—Je fais de la peinture, je joue de la musique et je fais de la danse.

—Est-ce que tu aimes venir ici?
—Oui.
—Pourquoi?
—Parce que c'est sympathique.
—Et à quoi est-ce que tu joues?
—Au ping-pong, au tennis, et puis au volley.

Au revoir, Créteil.

LEÇON 15 Au Café de l'Univers

PE AUDIO

CD 3, Track 9

Compréhension orale, p. 216

Où vas-tu après les cours?

Est-ce que tu vas directement chez toi?

Valérie, elle, ne va pas directement chez elle.

Ella va au Café de l'Univers avec ses copines Fatima et Zaïna.

Elle vient souvent ici avec elles.

À la table de Valérie la conversation est toujours très animée.

De quoi parlent les filles aujourd'hui?

Est-ce qu'elles parlent de l'examen d'histoire? du problème de maths? de la classe de sciences?

Non!

Est-ce qu'elles parlent du week-end prochain? des vacances?

Non plus!

Est-ce qu'elles parlent du nouveau copain de Marie-Claire? de la cousine de Pauline? des amis de Véronique?

Pas du tout!

Aujourd'hui, les filles parlent d'un sujet beaucoup plus important! Elles parlent du nouveau prof d'anglais! (C'est un jeune professeur américain. Il est très intéressant, très amusant, très sympathique . . .et surtout il est très mignon!)

CD 3, Track 10

Écoutez et répétez., p. 216

You will now hear a paused version of the dialogue. Listen to the speaker and repeat right after he or she has completed the sentence.

Prononciation, p. 223

CD 3, Track 11

Les voyelles /ø/ et /œ/

Écoutez: deux neuf

The letters "eu" and "oeu" represent vowel sounds that do not exist in English but that are not very hard to pronounce.

Répétez: /ø/ #   deux # eux # je veux # je peux # un peu # jeux # il pleut # un euro # Tu peux aller chez eux. #

/œ/ #   neuf # soeur # heure # professeur # jeune # Ma soeur arrive à neuf heures. #

À votre tour!

CD 3, Track 12

1. Conversation, p. 224

Listen to the conversation. *Écoutez la conversation entre Henri et Stéphanie.*

HENRI: Salut, Stéphanie! D'où viens-tu?

STÉPHANIE: Du supermarché.

HENRI: Et où vas-tu maintenant?

STÉPHANIE: Je rentre chez moi.

HENRI: Tu ne veux pas venir au cinéma avec moi?

STÉPHANIE: Je ne peux pas. Je dois étudier.

HENRI: Ah bon? Pourqoui?

STÉPHANIE: J'ai un examen d'anglais lundi.

CD 3, Track 13

2. Créa-dialogue, p. 224

Listen to some sample *Créa-dialogues. Écoutez les conversations.*

Modèle: —Où vas-tu?
    —Je vais chez Jean-Claude. Tu viens?

—Ça dépend. Qu'est-ce que tu vas
faire chez lui?
—Nous allons jouer au ping-pong.
—D'accord, je viens!

Maintenant, écoutez le dialogue numéro 1.

—Où vas-tu?
—Je vais chez Françoise. Tu viens?
—Ça dépend! Qu'est-ce que tu vas
faire chez elle?
—Nous allons regarder la télé.
—D'accord, je viens!

WORKBOOK AUDIO

Section 1. Je viens de . . .

CD 9, Track 17

A. Écoutez et répétez., p. 131

You will hear sentences containing forms of
the irregular verb "venir." Listen and repeat
where the following people are coming from.

1. Je viens du café. #
2. Tu viens du cinéma. #
3. Elle vient de la plage. #
4. Nous venons de la piscine. #
5. Vous venez du supermarché. #
6. Elles viennent du musée. #

CD 9, Track 18

B. Questions et réponses, p. 131

Now you will hear people asking you if you
are going to certain places. Answer each
question by saying that you are coming from
that place.

Modèle: Tu vas au café? # Non, je viens
du café.

Commençons.

1. Tu vas au cinéma? # Non, je viens du
cinéma.
2. Tu vas à la piscine? # Non, je viens de
la piscine.
3. Tu vas au musée? # Non, je viens
du musée.
4. Tu vas à la bibliothèque? # Non, je
viens de la bibliothèque.
5. Tu vas au restaurant? # Non, je viens
du restaurant.
6. Tu vas à l'école? Non, je viens de
l'école.

Section 2. Les sports et la musique

CD 9, Track 19

C. Compréhension orale, p. 131

The pictures in your Workbook show
different sports, games, and musical
instruments. You will hear ten sentences
which mention activities involving these
items. Match each sentence you hear to the
corresponding picture by writing its number
in the appropriate box.

Commençons.

1. Tu veux jouer au tennis? #
2. J'aime bien jouer de la guitare. #
3. Est-ce que tu joues aux échecs? #
4. Ma soeur joue de la flûte. #
5. Mon cousin joue de la batterie. #
6. Mon oncle joue de la clarinette. #
7. À l'école, les élèves jouent au basket. #
8. Tu veux jouer aux cartes avec nous? #
9. Est-ce que vous jouez du violon? #
10. Mes cousins aiment jouer aux dames. #

Now check your responses. You should have
written a-2, b-4, c-7, d-6, e-5, f-3, g-10, h-8, i-9,
j-1.

CD 9, Track 20

D. Questions et réponses, p. 131

Now it is your turn to say what people are
doing. Look at the pictures in your
Workbook and answer the questions
accordingly. Then listen for the
confirmation.

Modèle: Est-ce que Paul joue au tennis ou au
ping-pong?
Il joue au ping-pong.

1. Est-ce qu'il joue au volley ou au tennis?
   Il joue au tennis.
2. Est-ce qu'il joue au volley ou au basket? #
   Il joue au basket.
3. Est-ce qu'elle joue au volley ou au foot? #
   Elle joue au volley.
4. Est-ce qu'il joue au foot ou au baseball? #
   Il joue au baseball.
5. Est-ce qu'il joue au foot ou au basket? #
   Il joue au foot.

Section 3. Les pronoms accentués

CD 9, Track 21

E. Écoutez et répétez., p. 132

You will hear what various people do at home. Listen and repeat each sentence, paying attention to the stress pronouns.

Commençons.

Moi, je suis chez moi. #
Toi, tu restes chez toi. #
Lui, il étudie chez lui. #
Elle, elle travaille chez elle. #
Nous, nous dînons chez nous. #
Vous, vous mangez chez vous. #
Eux, ils regardent la télé chez eux. #
Elles, elles mangent une pizza chez elles. #

CD 9, Track 22

F. Parlez., p. 132

Now you will hear pronouns or names of people. Say that each person is going home.

Modèle: TOI # Tu vas chez toi.
JEAN-PAUL # Jean-Paul va chez lui.

Commençons.

1. Stéphanie # Stéphanie va chez elle.
2. Nicolas # Nicolas va chez lui.
3. Vous # Vous allez chez vous.
4. Nous # Nous allons chez nous.
5. Alice et Véronique # Alice et Véronique vont chez elles.

6. Pierre et François # Pierre et François vont chez eux.
7. Moi # Je vais chez moi.
8. Mon cousin # Mon cousin va chez lui.

Section 4. Conversations

CD 9, Track 23

G. La réponse logique, p. 132

You will hear a series of short questions, each one read twice. In your Workbook, circle the letter (a, b, or c) corresponding to the most logical answer.

Commençons.

1. Où allez-vous? #
2. D'où viens-tu? #
3. Quel est ton sport préféré? #
4. Tu joues d'un instrument de musique? #
5. Tu joues aux dames? #
6. Mathieu est à la maison?
7. Tu vas chez toi? #
8. Ton frère a une voiture de sport? #

Now check your answers. You should have circled 1-b, 2-b, 3-c, 4-b, 5-a, 6-a, 7-a, and 8-c.

Section 5. Dictée

CD 9, Track 24

H. Écoutez et écrivez., p. 132

You will hear a short dialogue spoken twice. First, listen carefully to what the people are saying. The second time you hear the dialogue, fill in the missing words.

Écoutez.

—Est-ce que ton copain est chez lui?
—Non, il est au cinéma avec son frère.
—À quelle heure est-ce qu'ils reviennent du cinéma?
—À six heures.
—Et qu'est-ce qu'ils vont faire après?
—Ils rentrent dîner chez eux.

Listen again and fill in the missing words.

B L E U

LESSON 15 QUIZ

Part I: Listening

CD 15, Track 3

A. Conversations

You will hear a series of short conversations between Éric and Stéphanie. Listen to each conversation carefully. Then answer the corresponding questions on your answer sheet by circling the appropriate letter (a, b, or c). You will hear each conversation twice.

Let's begin.

1. ÉRIC: D'où viens-tu?
    STÉPHANIE: Je reviens de la bibliothèque.

2. STÉPHANIE: Tu vas à la piscine?
    ÉRIC: Non, je rentre chez moi.

3. STÉPHANIE: Où vas-tu?
    ÉRIC: Je vais chez une copine.
    STÉPHANIE: Qu'est-ce que vous allez faire?
    ÉRIC: Nous allons jouer aux dames.

4. STÉPHANIE: C'est ton frère sur la photo?
    ÉRIC: Non, ce n'est pas lui.
    STÉPHANIE: Qui est-ce alors?
    ÉRIC: C'est moi!

5. ÉRIC: Où est ton cousin?
    STÉPHANIE: Il est chez lui.
    ÉRIC: Qu'est-ce qu'il fait?
    STÉPHANIE: Il regarde un match à la télé.

Nom _____

Classe _____ Date _____

Discovering
FRENCH *Nouveau!*

BLEU

Unité 5
Leçon 15
Lesson Quiz

QUIZ 15

PART I: LISTENING

A. Conversations (30 points)

You will hear a series of short conversations between Éric and Stéphanie. Listen to each conversation carefully. Then answer the corresponding questions on your answer sheet by circling the appropriate letter (a, b, or c). You will hear each conversation twice.

1. What is Éric asking Stéphanie?
   a. Where she is going.
   b. Where she is coming from.
   c. If she is going to the library.

2. Where is Éric going?
   a. Home.
   b. To the pool.
   c. To a neighbor's house.

3. What is Éric going to do?
   a. To listen to CDs.
   b. To play checkers.
   c. To go to a concert with a friend.

4. Who is the person in the picture?
   a. Éric.
   b. Éric's brother.
   c. A friend of Stéphanie's.

5. Where is Stéphanie's cousin?
   a. At home.
   b. In the garden.
   c. At the soccer stadium.

PART II: WRITING

B. La boum (16 points)

Say how or with whom the following people are coming to the party. Complete the sentences with the appropriate forms of **venir**.

1. Nous _____ avec des copains.

2. Je _____ en bus.

3. Janine _____ avec Élodie.

4. Thomas et Mélanie _____ en voiture.

Nom _____

Classe _____ Date _____

C. Loisirs (12 points)

Complete the following sentences with the appropriate words.

1. Je joue _____ piano.

2. Philippe joue _____ cartes.

3. Vous jouez _____ clarinette.

4. Nous jouons _____ baseball.

D. À la maison (18 points)

Everyone is home tonight. Complete the following sentences with the appropriate stress pronouns.

1. Marc rentre chez _____.

2. Pauline est chez _____.

3. Je joue aux jeux vidéo chez _____.

4. Nous dînons chez _____.

5. Isabelle et Alice sont chez _____.

6. Antoine et François vont chez _____.

E. Expression personnelle (24 points)

Answer the following questions in French. Write complete sentences.

• In general, at what time do you come home?

_____

• What sport(s) do you play?

_____

• What musical instrument would you like to play?

_____

• What game do you and your friends like to play?

_____

Nom _____

Classe _____ Date _____

Discovering FRENCH *Nouveau!*

B L E U

Unité 5
Leçon 16
Workbook TE

LEÇON 16 Mes voisins

LISTENING ACTIVITIES

Section 1. La famille

A. Écoutez et répétez.

la famille

les grands-parents	le grand-père	la grand-mère
les parents	le père	la mère
	le mari	la femme
les enfants	un enfant	une enfant
	le frère	la soeur
	le fils	la fille
des parents	l'oncle	la tante
	le cousin	la cousine

B. Compréhension orale

a. __1__ la grand-mère d'Olivier

b. __4__ la mère d'Olivier

c. __4__ la tante Alice

d. __4__ le mari de tante Alice

e. __2__ l'oncle Édouard

f. __4__ le père d'Olivier

g. __4__ les cousins d'Olivier

h. __3__ Olivier

1.

2.

3.

4.

Nom _____

Classe _____ Date _____

C. Questions et réponses

▶ —Qui est Éric Vidal?
   —**C'est le cousin de Frédéric.**

François Mallet: C'est le père de Frédéric.
Suzanne Mallet: C'est la grand-mère de Frédéric.
Isabelle Vidal: C'est la tante de Frédéric.
Catherine Vidal: C'est la cousine de Frédéric.
Véronique Mallet: C'est la soeur de Frédéric.
Maurice Vidal: C'est l'oncle de Frédéric.
Albert Mallet: C'est le grand-père de Frédéric.
Martine Mallet: C'est la mère de Frédéric.

Section 2. Les adjectifs possessifs

D. Écoutez et répétez.

mon copain, ma copine, mes amis

ton père, ta soeur, tes parents

son baladeur, sa chaîne hi-fi, ses CD

notre maison, nos voisins

votre école, vos profs

leur tante, leurs cousins

E. Écoutez et parlez.

Modèle: une guitare   **C'est ma guitare.**

un baladeur   C'est mon baladeur.
une chaîne hi-fi   C'est ma chaîne hi-fi.
des livres   Ce sont mes livres.
un portable   C'est mon portable.
des CD   Ce sont mes CD.

Modèle: une maison   **C'est notre maison.**

une voiture   C'est notre voiture.
un ordinateur   C'est notre ordinateur.
des photos   Ce sont nos photos.

Nom _____

Classe _____ Date _____

Discovering
FRENCH *Nouveau!*

B L E U

Unité 5
Leçon 16

Workbook TE

F. Parlez.

Modèle: C'est la voiture de Marc?   **Oui, c'est sa voiture.**

Oui, c'est son baladeur.

Oui, c'est son portable.

Oui, c'est sa guitare.

Modèle: C'est la maison de tes voisins?   **Oui, c'est leur maison.**

Oui, c'est leur voiture.

Oui, ce sont leurs CD.

Oui, ce sont leurs photos.

G. Compréhension orale

		Modèles	1	2	3	4	5	6	7	8	9	10
A:		✔	✔		✔					✔		✔
B:			✔		✔		✔	✔	✔	✔		✔

Section 3. Dictée

H. Écoutez et écrivez.

Modèle: Eh bien, voilà. C'est _ma_ maison.

1. Et ça, c'est la maison des voisins. C'est _leur_ maison.

2. Ça, c'est _notre_ voiture. Et ça c'est leur voiture.

3. Voici _ma_ mobylette.

4. Et voilà la mobylette de mon frère. C'est _sa_ mobylette.

5. Voici _notre_ cuisine.

6. Voici _ma_ chambre.

7. Et voici la chambre de mes parents. C'est _leur_ chambre.

8. Voici la chambre de ma soeur. C'est _sa_ chambre.

9. Ah, mais ça, ce n'est pas son baladeur! C'est _mon_ baladeur.

Nom _____

Classe _____ Date _____

WRITING ACTIVITIES

A 1. La consigne *(The check room)*

The following objects have been left at the check room, tagged with their owner's names. Identify each item.

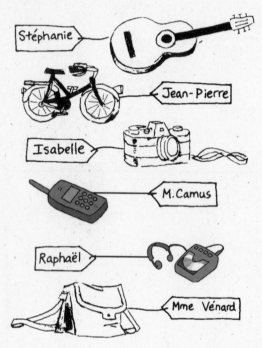

▶ C'est la guitare de Stéphanie.

1. C'est le vélo de Jean-Pierre.

2. C'est l'appareil-photo d'Isabelle.

3. C'est le portable de Monsieur Camus.

4. C'est le baladeur de Raphaël.

5. C'est le sac de Madame Vénard.

2. En famille

Look at the family tree and explain the relationships between the following people.

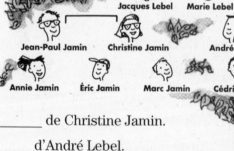

Jacques Lebel   Marie Lebel

Jean-Paul Jamin   Christine Jamin   André Lebel   Nathalie Lebel

Annie Jamin   Éric Jamin   Marc Jamin   Cédric Lebel   Catherine Lebel

▶ Jean-Paul Jamin est le mari _____ de Christine Jamin.

1. Nathalie Lebel est la femme _____ d'André Lebel.

2. Jacques et Marie Lebel sont les grands-parents _____ de Cédric.

3. Marie Lebel est la mère _____ de Christine Jamin.

4. Éric et Marc sont les fils (les enfants) _____ de Christine Jamin.

5. Cédric est le cousin _____ d'Éric.

6. Catherine est la cousine _____ de Marc.

7. Catherine est la fille _____ d'André et Nathalie Lebel.

8. Jean-Paul Jamin est l'oncle _____ de Cédric et de Catherine.

9. Nathalie Lebel est la tante _____ d'Annie Jamin.

Nom _____

Classe _____ Date _____

Discovering
FRENCH
Nouveau!

BLEU

Unité 5
Leçon 16
Workbook TE

B 3. En vacances

The following people are spending their vacations with friends or family. Complete the sentences below with **son, sa,** or **ses**, as appropriate.

1. Guillaume voyage avec _sa_____ soeur et _ses_____ parents.

2. Juliette visite Paris avec _son_____ frère et _ses_____ cousines.

3. Paul va chez _son_____ ami Alain.

4. Sandrine est chez _son_____ amie Sophie.

5. En juillet, Jean-Paul va chez _ses_____ grands-parents.

   En août, il va chez _sa_____ tante Marthe. En septembre,

   il va chez _ses_____ amis anglais.

6. Hélène va chez _son_____ grand-père. Après (*afterwards*), elle

   va chez _son_____ oncle François.

B/C 4. Pourquoi pas?

The following people are not engaged in certain activities because they do not have certain things. Complete the sentences with **son, sa, ses, leur,** or **leurs** and an appropriate object from the box. Be logical.

radio	**voiture**	*ordinateur*	**mobylette**
stylos	**raquettes**	**livres**	portable

▶ Isabelle et Cécile n'étudient pas. Elles n'ont pas _leurs livres_____.

1. Pierre et Julien ne jouent pas au tennis. Ils n'ont pas _leurs raquettes_____.

2. Philippe ne va pas en ville. Il n'a pas _sa mobylette (sa voiture)_____.

3. Alice et Claire n'écoutent pas le concert. Elles n'ont pas _leur radio_____.

4. Madame Imbert ne travaille pas. Elle n'a pas _son ordinateur_____.

5. Mes parents ne voyagent pas. Ils n'ont pas _leur voiture_____.

6. Les élèves n'écrivent pas (*are not writing*). Ils n'ont pas _leurs stylos_____.

7. Élodie ne téléphone pas. Elle n'a pas _son portable_____.

URB
p. 107

Discovering French, Nouveau! Bleu

Unité 5, Leçon 16
Workbook

141

Nom _____

Classe _____ Date _____

Discovering
FRENCH
Nouveau!

B L E U

5. Le week-end

On weekends we like to do things with our friends and relatives. Complete the sentences below with the appropriate possessive adjectives.

▶ Nous faisons une promenade en voiture avec *nos* parents.

1. Isabelle et Francine vont au cinéma avec *leurs* cousins.

2. Je joue au tennis avec *mes* copains.

3. Tu dînes chez *ton* oncle.

4. Philippe et Marc vont au restaurant avec *leurs* copines.

5. Hélène fait une promenade à vélo avec *son* frère.

6. Nous téléphonons à *notre* grand-mère.

7. Vous allez au musée avec *votre* oncle.

8. Nous jouons aux cartes avec *nos* amis.

9. Vous visitez un musée avec *votre* soeur.

MUSEE PICASSO

MUSEE D'HISTOIRE ET D'ARCHEOLOGIE

D 6. La course cycliste

Say how the following people finished the bicycle race.

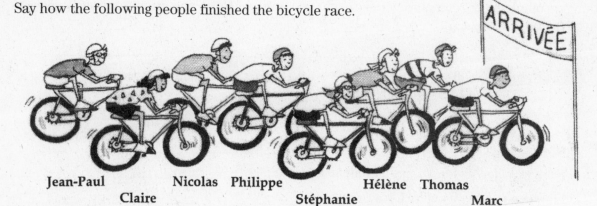

Jean-Paul   Nicolas Philippe   Hélène Thomas
       Claire   Stéphanie   Marc

ARRIVÉE

▶ Nicolas *est sixième* .   4. Hélène *est troisième* .

1. Philippe *est cinquième* .   5. Jean-Paul *est huitième* .

2. Claire *est septième* .   6. Thomas *est deuxième* .

3. Marc *est premier* .   7. Stéphanie *est quatrième* .

Nom _____

Classe _____ Date _____

Discovering
FRENCH *Nouveau!*
BLEU

Unité 5
Leçon 16
Workbook TE

7. Communication: La famille de mes amis (sample answers)

Think of two of your friends. For each one, write four sentences describing his/her family.
(If you wish, you can describe the families of imaginary friends.)

▶ Mon copain s'appelle Tom .

   Sa sœur s'appelle Wendy.

   Son père travaille dans un magasin.

   Sa mère travaille dans un hôpital.

   Ses cousins habitent à Cincinnati.

• Mon copain s'appelle Martin .

   Sa mère travaille dans un musée.

   Son frère s'appelle Joe.

   Sa grand-mère habite avec eux.

   Son oncle voyage souvent.

• Ma copine s'appelle Nancy .

   Son père travaille dans un restaurant.

   Sa mère travaille dans un magasin.

   Sa sœur s'appelle Joan.

   Ses cousines habitent à Denver.

Discovering French, Nouveau! Bleu

URB
p. 109

Unité 5, Leçon 16
Workbook
143

Nom _____

Classe _____ Date _____

Discovering
FRENCH
Nouveau!

BLEU

Unité 5
Leçon 16

Activités pour tous TE

LEÇON 16   Mes voisins

A

Activité 1   C'est à qui?

Fill in the blanks with **de, du, de la, de l', d',** or **des.**

1. C'est le portable _de_ Robert.

2. C'est le chien _de la_ voisine.

3. Ce sont les livres _des_ étudiants.

4. C'est le stylo _du_ prof.

5. C'est la mobylette _de l'_ ami _d'_ Amélie.

Activité 2   C'est à qui?

Fill in the blanks with the correct adjectives and nouns.

mon / ma	ton / ta	son / sa	notre	votre	leur

1. (moi)   C'est _mon_ _stylo_.

2. (toi)   C'est _ta_ _guitare_.

3. (lui)   C'est _sa_ _moto_.

4. (eux)   C'est _leur_ _chat_.

5. (nous)   C'est _notre_ _ordinateur_.

Activité 3   Qui est le gagnant?

Someone got disqualified in the race. Adjust the order of finish by moving everyone up one place.

1. —Patrick arrive troisième? —Non, il arrive *cinquième /* *deuxième.*

2. —Aude arrive huitième? —Non, elle arrive *septième / sixième.*

3. —Georges arrive deuxième? —Non, il arrive *quatrième /* *premier.*

4. —Monique arrive dixième? —Non, elle arrive *onzième /* *neuvième.*

5. —Chantal arrive cinquième? —Non, elle arrive *quatrième / troisième.*

Who wins? _Georges_   Who's last? _Monique_

Nom _____

Classe _____ Date _____

B

Activité 1 La possession

Using **de**, identify who owns what belonging.

Modèle: 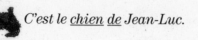 C'est le <u>chien</u> <u>de</u> Jean-Luc.

1. C'est l' <u>ordinateur</u> <u>de</u> Robert.

2. C'est la <u>voiture</u> <u>de la</u> voisine.

3. Ce sont les <u>portables</u> <u>des</u> étudiants.

4. C'est la <u>calculatrice</u> <u>du</u> prof.

5. C'est le <u>sac</u> <u>d'</u> Amélie.

Activité 2 Un jeu de cartes

Fill in the blanks with the correct possessives and with **de**, following the example.

Un as   La reine de pique   Le dix de coeur   Le cinq de carreau

Modèle: C'est _____ton_____ as _____de_____ trèfle.
(toi)

1. C'est <u>mon</u> as <u>de</u> pique.
(moi)

2. C'est <u>son</u> as <u>de</u> carreau.
(lui)

3. C'est <u>ton</u> as <u>de</u> coeur.
(toi)

4. C'est <u>ma</u> reine <u>de</u> pique.
(moi)

5. C'est <u>votre</u> reine <u>de</u> coeur.
(vous)

6. Ce sont <u>vos</u> cinq et dix <u>de</u> trèfle.
(vous)

Activité 3 Qui est le gagnant?

The performances of the five long jump competitors are in parentheses. Put them in order so that medals can be awarded.

1. Karine (2 m 80)   : <u>quatrième</u>
2. Philippe (3 m 50) : <u>troisième</u>
3. Yannick (3 m 80) : <u>premier</u>
4. Sandrine (3 m 75) : <u>deuxième</u>

Or *(Gold)* <u>Yannick</u>   Argent *(Silver)* <u>Sandrine</u>   Bronze <u>Philippe</u>

premier

deuxième

troisième

quatrième

cinquième

Nom _____

Classe _____ Date _____

Discovering
FRENCH *Nouveau!*

B L E U

Unité 5
Leçon 16

Activités pour tous TE

C

Activité 1 C'est à qui?

Everybody's belongings got mixed up at the summer camp. Answer the question **C'est à qui?**

Modèle: C'est l'affiche d'Alexandra.

(Alexandra)

1. (Alain)   *C'est la guitare d'Alain.*

2. (Brigitte)   *C'est la raquette de Brigitte.*

3. (Pascal)   *C'est l'appareil-photo de Pascal.*

4. (Ming)   *C'est le baladeur de Ming.*

5. (Serge)   *C'est le violon de Serge.*

Activité 2 Mon arbre généalogique

Frédéric is telling you about his family members. Fill in the blanks with the correct possessive adjectives (**mon, ton, son...**).

1. *C'est ma tante.*

2. *C'est mon grand-père*

3. *C'est ma grand-mère.*

4. *C'est ma soeur.*

5. *C'est mon cousin.*

6. *Ce sont mes parents.*

C'est moi!

Activité 3 Dates de naissances

The Dumonts have five children. They are listed below with their birthdates. Write the ordinal number that indicates in what order each was born.

1. Frédéric, 25/01/82 *deuxième*

2. Sylvie, 10/04/86 *quatrième*

3. Sandrine, 14/06/84 *troisième*

4. Anne, 02/09/80 *première*

5. Patrick, 30/11/90 *cinquième*

URB
p. 113

Unité 5
Leçon 16

Lesson Plans

Discovering
FRENCH
Nouveau!

BLEU

LEÇON 16 Mes voisins, page 226

Objectives

Communicative Functions and Topics	To talk about possessions
	To identify and describe family members
	To express doubt
Linguistic Goals	To use ordinal numbers and possessive adjectives
	To indicate possession with *de*
	To pronounce vowels /o/ and /ɔ/
Cultural Goals	To learn about places in Paris
	To be aware of the popularity of French and American films in France

Motivation and Focus

❏ Ask students to describe the apartment building on page 226. How is this building similar to local homes or apartment buildings? How is it different?

Presentation and Explanation

❏ *Lesson Opener:* Use **Overhead Transparency** 34 with SETTING THE STAGE, pages 226–227 of the TE. Play **Audio CD** 3, Tracks 14–15 or read aloud the monologue, page 226. Then ask students to read to determine where the people live in the building.

❏ *Notes culturelles:* Have students read *Les animaux domestiques en France*, page 227.

❏ *Grammar A:* Explain the use of *de* to talk about possessions, page 228. Point out contractions with *de* and have students talk about things possessed by others.

❏ *Vocabulaire:* Introduce family vocabulary, page 229, with **Overhead Transparency** 8, or **Audio CD** 3, Track 16. Model family relationship terms and have students repeat. Then guide students to use the terms to identify family members.

❏ *Grammar B and C:* Introduce possessive adjectives. Point out that possessive adjectives need to agree with the nouns they describe. Have students practice the examples on pages 230 and 232. Present the box on expressing a doubt on page 231.

❏ *Grammar D:* Present ordinal numbers, page 233. Model and have students repeat. Point out the LANGUAGE NOTES information in the TE margin.

❏ *Prononciation:* Explain pronunciation of /o/ and /ɔ/ using the ideas in PRONUNCIATION NOTES, page 233 of the TE. Model or play **Audio CD** 3, Track 17 and have students repeat the words.

Guided Practice and Checking Understanding

❏ Use **Overhead Transparency** 8 and the activity on pages A57–A58 to practice describing family members and using possessive adjectives. Practice using ordinal numbers and talking about an apartment building with Transparency 34 and the activities on pages A96–A97.

❏ Use **Audio CD** 9, Tracks 25–32 or the **Audioscript** with **Workbook** Listening Activities A–H, pages 137–139, to check listening comprehension.

❏ Use the **Video** or **Videoscript** using pages 125–127 in **Video Activities**.

❏ Practice talking about possession using the COMPREHENSION ACTIVITY on page 230 of the TE.

Independent Practice

❏ Have students do the activities on pages 228–233. Do 1–3, 5, 6, and 9–11 as homework. Model and have students do 4, 7, and 8 as PAIR PRACTICE.

Discovering
FRENCH *Nouveau!*

B L E U

Unité 5
Leçon 16
Lesson Plans

❑ Use **Communipak** *Tête à tête* 4, pages 159–160, or **Video Activities** page 128 for oral practice about families.
❑ Have students do the activities in **Activités pour tous,** pages 83–85.

Monitoring and Adjusting

❑ Assign **Workbook** Writing Activities 1–7 on pages 140–143.
❑ Monitor use of possessive adjectives as students work on the practice activities. Point out the grammar and vocabulary boxes, pages 228–233. Explain the information in LANGUAGE and PRONUNCIATION NOTES in the TE margins.

End-of-Lesson Activities

❑ *À votre tour!:* Students can prepare and practice Activities 1–3, pages 234 and 235. Use **Audio CD** 3, Tracks 18–19 with Activities 1–2. Assign Activities 4 and 5 for written homework.

Review

❑ Have students review the information they learned in this unit by completing the *Test de contrôle* activities on pages 236–237. Encourage students to use the page references in the **Review** . . . tabs to verify/clarify grammar and vocabulary.

Reteaching

❑ Use any appropriate activities from the **Workbook** for reteaching as necessary.
❑ Assign the **Video** to students for review.

Assessment

❑ Use **Quiz 16** on pages 137–138 after completing the lesson. Give Unit Test 5 (Form A or B) on pages 177–185 of **Unit Resources**. For assessment of specific language skills, select the appropriate **Performance Tests**. The **Test Generator** can be used to adjust tests and quizzes to meet the class's specific needs.

Extension and Enrichment

❑ Play the GAME about possessions on pages 232–233 of the TE.

Summary and Closure

❑ Help students summarize the grammar and vocabulary of the lesson. Then show **Overhead Transparency** 34 and ask them to prepare a short description of one of the families in the picture, using as much of the content of the lesson as possible.
❑ Do PORTFOLIO ASSESSMENT on page 235 of the TE.

End-of-Unit Activities

❑ *Entracte 5:* Follow the PRE- and POST-READING suggestions and teaching tips in the TE margins for *Entracte 5* pages 240–245. Remind them to use cognates as they read.
❑ *Reading and Culture Activities:* Do **Workbook** pages 145–148.

Discovering
FRENCH *Nouveau!*

B L E U

LEÇON 16 Mes voisins, page 226

Block Scheduling (5 days to complete – including unit test)

Objectives

Communicative Functions and Topics
To talk about possessions
To identify and describe family members
To express doubt

Linguistic Goals
To use ordinal numbers and possessive adjectives
To indicate possession with de
To pronounce vowels /o/ and /ɔ/

Cultural Goals
To learn about places in Paris
To be aware of the popularity of French and American films in France

Block Scheduling

Fun Break Have students bring in photos of their family members. Have them tape their name and the person's relationship to them on the back of each photo. Then have the class guess the identity of each person in the photographs. ■

Day 1

Motivation and Focus

❑ Ask students to describe the apartment building on page 226. How is this building similar to local homes or apartment buildings? How is it different?

Presentation and Explanation

❑ *Lesson Opener:* Use **Overhead Transparency** 34 with SETTING THE STAGE, pages 226–227 of the TE. Play **Audio CD** 3, Tracks 14–15 or read aloud the monologue, page 226. Then ask students to read to determine where the people live in the building.
❑ *Notes culturelles:* Have students read *Les animaux domestiques en France*, page 227.
❑ *Grammar A:* Explain the use of *de* to talk about possessions, page 228. Point out contractions with *de* and have students talk about things possessed by others.
❑ *Vocabulaire:* Introduce family vocabulary, page 229, with **Overhead Transparency** 8, or **Audio CD** 3, Track 16. Model family relationship terms and have students repeat. Then guide students to use the terms to identify family members.
❑ *Grammar B* and *C:* Introduce possessive adjectives. Point out that possessive adjectives need to agree with the nouns they describe. Have students practice the examples on pages 230 and 232. Present the box on expressing a doubt on page 231.
❑ *Grammar D:* Present ordinal numbers, page 233. Model and have students repeat. Point out the LANGUAGE NOTES information in the TE margin.
❑ *Prononciation:* Explain pronunciation of /o/ and /ɔ/ using the ideas in PRONUNCIATION NOTES, page 233 of the TE. Model or play **Audio CD** 3, Track 17 and have students repeat the words.

Discovering
FRENCH
Nouveau!

B L E U

Unité 5
Leçon 16

Block Scheduling
Lesson Plans

Guided Practice and Checking Understanding

❏ Use **Overhead Transparency** 8 and the activity on pages A57–A58 to practice describing family members and using possessive adjectives. Practice using ordinal numbers and talking about an apartment building with Transparency 34 and the activities on pages A96–A97.

❏ Use **Audio CD** 9, Tracks 25–32 or the **Audioscript** with **Workbook** Listening Activities A–H, pages 137–139 to check listening comprehension.

Day 2

Motivation and Focus

❏ Use the **Video** or **Videoscript** with pages 125–127 of **Video Activities**.
❏ Practice talking about possessions using the COMPREHENSION ACTIVITY on page 230 of the TE.

Independent Practice

❏ Have students do the activities on pages 228–233. Do 1–3, 5, 6, and 9–11 as homework. Model and have students do 4, 7, and 8 as PAIR PRACTICE.
❏ Use **Communipak** *Tête à tête* 4, pages 159–160, or **Video Activities** page 128 for oral practice about families.
❏ Have students do the activities in **Activités pour tous,** pages 83–85.

Monitoring and Adjusting

❏ Assign **Workbook** Writing Activities 1–7 on pages 140–143.
❏ Monitor use of possessive adjectives as students work on the practice activities. Point out the grammar and vocabulary boxes, pages 228–233. Explain the information in LANGUAGE and PRONUNCIATION NOTES in the TE margin.

Day 3

End-of-Lesson Activities

❏ *À votre tour!:* Students can prepare and practice Activities 1–3, pages 234 and 235. Use **Audio CD** 3, Tracks 18–19 with Activities 1–2. Assign Activities 4 and 5 for written homework.

Review

❏ Have students review the information they learned in this unit by completing the *Test de contrôle* activities on pages 236–237. Encourage students to use the page references in the **Review** . . . tabs to verify/clarify grammar and vocabulary.

Reteaching (as needed)

❏ Use any appropriate activities from the **Workbook** for reteaching as necessary.
❏ Assign the **Video** to students for review.

BLEU

Extension and Enrichment (as desired)

❏ Play the GAME about possessions on pages 232–233 of the TE.
❏ For expansion activities, direct students to www.classzone.com.
❏ Have students do the **Block Schedule Activity** on page 116.
❏ Use **Block Scheduling Copymasters,** pages 121–128.

Summary and Closure

❏ Help students summarize the grammar and vocabulary of the lesson. Then show **Overhead Transparency** 34 and ask them to prepare a short description of one of the families in the picture, using as much of the content of the lesson as possible.
❏ Do PORTFOLIO ASSESSMENT on page 235 of the TE.

Assessment

❏ Use **Quiz 16** on page 137–138 after completing the lesson. The **Test Generator** can be used to adjust the quiz to meet the class's specific needs.

Day 4

End-of-Unit Activities

Note: These activities may be done at the end of the unit, or at any time that seems appropriate during the unit.
❏ *Entracte 5:* Follow the PRE-READING and POST-READING suggestions and teaching tips in the TE margins for *Entracte 5*, pages 240–245. Remind students to use cognates as they read.
❏ *Reading and Culture Activities:* Do **Workbook** pages 145–148.

Day 5

Assessment

❏ Give Unit Test 5 (Form A or B) on pages 177–185 of **Unit Resources**.
❏ For assessment of specific language skills, select the appropriate **Performance Tests**. Any of the test questions can be modified using the **Test Generator**.

Notes

Nom _____

Classe _____ Date _____

Discovering
FRENCH *Nouveau!*

B L E U

LEÇON 16 Mes voisins, pages 226–227

Materials Checklist

- **Student Text**
- **Audio CD** 3, Tracks 14–15
- **Video** 3 or **DVD** 2; Counter 21:28–25:47

Steps to Follow

- Before you read the passage on p. 226, read the *Compréhension* questions on p. 227. They will help you understand the passage and the audio.
- Read the passage on p. 226 before you listen to the audio or watch the video.
- Watch **Video** 3 or **DVD** 2; Counter 21:28–25:47, or listen to **Audio CD** 3, Tracks 14–15.
- Answer the *Compréhension* questions (p. 227) on a separate sheet of paper.
- Read *Comparaisons culturelles* (p. 227).
- Read the *Note culturelle* (p. 227). Write any expressions you do not understand on a separate sheet of paper.

If You Don't Understand . . .

- Watch the **Video** or **DVD** in a quiet place. Try to stay focused. If you get lost, stop the **Video** or **DVD**. Replay it and find your place.
- Listen to the **CD** in a quiet place. Try to stay focused. If you get lost, stop the **CD**. Replay it and find your place.
- Repeat aloud with the audio. Try to sound like the people on the recording.
- On a separate sheet of paper, write down the words that are underlined in the text. Check for meaning.
- Say aloud anything you write. Make sure you understand everything you say.
- Write down any questions so that you can ask your partner or your teacher later.

Self-Check

Answer the following true/false questions on a separate sheet of paper. If the statement is false, give the correct answer.

1. L'immeuble de Frédéric a six étages.
2. Les Lacroche habitent au cinquième étage.
3. Frédéric pense que Mademoiselle Ménard est un peu bizarre.
4. Les Français n'aiment pas les animaux domestiques.
5. Il y a 60 millions d'animaux domestiques en France.

Answers

1. True. 2. False. Les Lacroche habitent au sixième étage. 3. False. Le père de Frédéric pense que Mademoiselle Ménard est un peu bizarre. 4. False. Les Français adorent les animaux domestiques. 5. False. Il y a 42 millions d'animaux domestiques en France.

Nom _____

Classe _____ Date _____ _____

Discovering FRENCH *Nouveau!*

BLEU

A. La possession avec *de,* pages 228–229

Materials Checklist

- **Student Text**
- **Audio CD** 3, Track 16; **CD** 9, Tracks 25–27
- **Workbook**

Steps to Follow

- Study *La possession avec de* (p. 228). Copy the model sentences and read them aloud. Underline the expressions showing possession with **de**.
- Complete Activities 1 and 2 in the text (p. 228). Write your answers in complete sentences on a separate sheet of paper. Underline the expressions showing possession with **de**.
- Read *Vocabulaire: La famille* (p. 229), then listen to **Audio CD** 3, Track 16.
- Copy the vocabulary list on a separate sheet of paper.
- Do Activity 3 in the text (p. 229).
- Do **Writing Activities** A 1, 2 in the **Workbook** (p. 140).
- Do **Listening Activities** A–C in the **Workbook** (pp. 137–138). Use **Audio CD** 9, Tracks 25–27.

If You Don't Understand . . .

- Reread the activity directions. Put the directions in your own words.
- Say aloud everything that you write. Be sure you understand what you are saying.
- Write down questions so that you can ask your partner or your teacher later.
- When writing a sentence, ask yourself, "What do I mean? What am I trying to say?"
- Listen to the **CDs** in a quiet place. Try to stay focused. If you get lost, stop the **CDs**. Replay them and find your place.
- Listen once without repeating. Then replay and repeat aloud with the audio. Try to sound like the people on the recording. Imitate their sounds and accents. Pause the **CD** if you need to.

Self-Check

Explain the relationships between the people below. Write complete sentences on a separate sheet of paper.

1. Anne / mère / Louise
2. Thomas / frère / Annette
3. Hélène / amie / Jacques
4. Paul / père / Pierre
5. Jeanne et Alice / cousines / Hélène
6. Michèle / tante / Carole
7. Nous / les grands-parents / Pauline

Answers

1. Anne est la mère de Louise. 2. Thomas est le frère d'Annette. 3. Hélène est l'amie de Jacques. 4. Paul est le père de Pierre. 5. Jeanne et Alice sont les cousines d'Hélène. 6. Michèle est la tante de Carole. 7. Nous sommes les grands-parents de Pauline.

Nom _____

Classe _____ Date _____

Discovering
FRENCH
Nouveau!

B L E U

Unité 5
Leçon 16

Absent Student
Copymasters

B. Les adjectifs possessifs: *mon, ton, son,* pages 230–231

Materials Checklist

- **Student Text**
- **Workbook**

Steps to Follow

- Study the hint *Learning about Language* (p. 230).
- Study *Les adjectifs possessifs:* **mon, ton, son** (p. 230). Write singular and plural forms of the masculine and feminine possessive adjectives on a separate sheet of paper.
- Study the liaisons of the feminine forms of the possessive adjectives (p. 230). Write the models on a separate sheet of paper and underline the liaisons, for example, **mon amie.**
- Do Activity 4 in the text (p. 231). Write the parts for both speakers in complete sentences on a separate sheet of paper.
- Do Activities 5 and 6 in the text (p. 231). Write the answers on a separate sheet of paper. Read them aloud. Underline the possessive adjectives, for examples, **Ta raquette est là-bas.**
- Study *Vocabulaire: Expression pour la conversation* (p. 231).
- Do Activity 7 in the text (p. 231). Write the dialogue on a separate sheet of paper. Read both parts aloud.
- Do **Writing Activities** B 3 and B/C 4 in the **Workbook** (p. 141).

If You Don't Understand . . .

- Reread the activity directions. Put the directions in your own words.
- Read the model several times. Be sure you understand it. Underline the new expressions, for example, **C'est <u>son</u> sac.**
- Say aloud everything that you write. Be sure you understand what you are saying.
- Write down questions so that you can ask your partner or your teacher later.
- When writing a sentence, ask yourself, "What do I mean? What am I trying to say?"

Self-Check

Say whether each item belongs to you or to Anne. Write complete sentences on a separate sheet of paper.

1. Est-ce que c'est ton CD? (oui)
2. Est-ce que c'est le vélo d'Anne? (oui)
3. Est-ce que c'est ta raquette de tennis? (oui)
4. Est-ce que c'est la montre d'Anne? (non)
5. Est-ce que ce sont les livres d'Anne? (oui)
6. Est-ce que c'est ton appareil-photo? (non)

Answers

1. Oui, c'est mon CD. 2. Oui, c'est son vélo. 3. Oui, c'est ma raquette de tennis. 4. Non, ce n'est pas sa montre. 5. Oui, ce sont ses livres. 6. Non, ce n'est pas mon appareil-photo.

Nom _____

Classe _____ Date _____

C. Les adjectifs possessifs: *notre, votre, leur,* page 232
D. Les nombres ordinaux, page 233

Materials Checklist

- **Student Text**
- **Audio CD** 3, Tracks 17–19; **CD** 9, Tracks 28–32
- **Video** 3 or **DVD** 2; Counter 21:28–24:27
- **Workbook**

Steps to Follow

- Study *Les adjectifs possessifs: **notre, votre, leur*** (p. 232). Copy the chart.
- Watch **Video** 3 or **DVD** 2; Counter 21:28–24:27.
- Do Activities 8, 9, and 10 in the text (p. 232). Write the answers in complete sentences. Underline the possessive pronouns in each sentence.
- Read the hint *Learning about Language* (p. 233). Study *Les nombres ordinaux* (p. 233). Write out the ordinal numbers in French from "first" to "eleventh."
- Do Activity 11 in the text (p. 233). Write your answers on a separate sheet of paper.
- Read the words in *Prononciation: Les voyelles /o/ et /ɔ/* (p. 233) before you listen to the audio. Listen to *Prononciation: /o/ and /ɔ/* on **Audio** CD 3, Track 17. Repeat what you hear.
- Do **Writing Activities** D 6, 7 in the **Workbook** (pp. 142–143).
- Do **Listening Activities** D–H in the **Workbook** (pp. 138–139). Use **Audio CD** 9, Tracks 28–32.
- Do Activities 1–5 of *À votre tour!* in the text (pp. 234–235). Use **Audio CD** 3, Tracks 18–19 with Activities 1–2.

If You Don't Understand . . .

- Watch the **Video** or **DVD** in a quiet place. Try to stay focused. If you get lost, stop the **Video** or **DVD**. Replay it and find your place.
- Listen to the **CDs** in a quiet place. Try to stay focused. If you get lost, stop the **CDs**. Replay them and find your place.
- Reread the activity directions. Put the directions in your own words.
- Read the model several times before beginning so you are certain what to do. Copy the model.
- Write down any questions so that you can ask your teacher or your partner later.

Self-Check

Provide the correct possessive adjective in each of the following sentences.

1. Alain va au cinéma avec . . . copine.
2. Jean et Alice dînent chez . . . grands-parents.
3. Nous avons une voiture et des vélos. Voilà . . . voiture et . . . vélos.
4. Vous avez un chien et des chats? Ah, voilà . . . chien et . . . chats!
5. Jeanne et Marie voyagent avec . . . père.

Answers

1. Alain va au cinéma avec sa copine. 2. Jean et Alice dînent chez leurs grands-parents. 3. Nous avons une voiture et des vélos. Voilà notre voiture et nos vélos. 4. Vous avez un chien et des chats? Ah, voilà votre chien et vos chats! 5. Jeanne et Marie voyagent avec leur père.

Nom

Classe _____ Date _____

Discovering FRENCH Nouveau!

BLEU

Unité 5
Leçon 16

Family Involvement

LEÇON 16   Mes voisins

La famille

Ask a family member to identify which person he or she is on a family tree in relation to you.

- First, explain your assignment.
- Model the pronunciation of the words under each picture. Point to the picture as you model the answers.
- Then, ask the question: **Qui es-tu?**
- After you get the answer, complete the sentence at the bottom of the page.

le grand-père   la grand-mère

le père — la mère   l'oncle   la tante

la fille   le fils   la cousine   le cousin

_____ est mon/ma _____.

Discovering
FRENCH
Nouveau!

BLEU

Nom _____

Classe _____ Date _____

Les amis

Ask a family member for the names of your neighbors (**nos voisins**) and for the name of one friend of your family member (**ton ami[e]**).

- First, explain your assignment.
- Model the pronunciation of the vocabulary words, and provide English equivalents.
- Ask the questions: **a) Comment s'appellent nos voisins?**
  b) Comment s'appelle ton ami(e)?
- When you have the answers, write your answers below.

a) _____.

b) _____.

Nom _____

Classe _____ Date _____

Discovering
FRENCH
Nouveau!

BLEU

Unité 5
Leçon 16
Video Activities

MODULE 16   Où habitez-vous?

Video 3, DVD 2

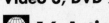 **16 Activité 1.** Où habitent les Français?
Counter 20:35–21:27

Where do French people live? As you listen to the video, circle the letter of the correct completion to each statement below.

1. Most French people in big cities live in . . .   a. houses   b. apartments

2. **Le rez-de-chaussée** is the . . . floor.   a. first   b. second

3. Apartment buildings are more modern in the . . .   a. cities   b. suburbs

16.1 Activité 2. La maison de Nathalie
Counter 21:28–22:29

As you watch the video, number the following statements from 1 to 9 in the order you hear them.

a. _____ Et ça, c'est la maison des voisins. C'est leur maison.

b. _____ Voici la chambre de ma soeur. C'est sa chambre.

c. _____ Voici ma mobylette.

d. _____ Eh bien, voilà. C'est ma maison.

e. _____ Et voici la chambre de mes parents. C'est leur chambre.

f. _____ Voici ma chambre.

g. _____ Et voilà la mobylette de mon frère. C'est sa mobylette.

h. _____ Ça, c'est notre voiture. Et ça, c'est leur voiture.

i. _____ Voici notre living.

Discovering
FRENCH
Nouveau!

B L E U

16.2 Activité 3. À qui est-ce?

Counter 22:30–23:27

To whom do different things belong? As you watch
the video segment, write the appropriate word in
the blanks below.

1. —C'est ta voiture?

   —Eh bien, oui, c'est _____ voiture.

2. —C'est votre voiture?

   —Euh, oui, c'est _____ voiture.

3. —C'est ton stylo?

   —Non, ce n'est pas _____ stylo!

4. —C'est ton ordinateur?

   —Ben, oui, c'est _____ ordinateur.

5. —C'est votre maison?

   —C'est _____ maison.

   —C'est _____ maison.

6. —C'est mon sandwich.

   —Non, ce n'est pas _____ sandwich. C'est mon sandwich!

   —Mais non. Ce n'est pas _____ sandwich. C'est mon sandwich!

7. —C'est ton copain?

   —Non, c'est le copain de _____ cousine.

16.3 Activité 4. La famille d'Olivier

Counter 23:28–24:27

Who are the people in Olivier's family pictures? Number the people listed below from 1 to 7 in
the order you hear Olivier identify them in the video.

a. _____ ma grand-mère

b. _____ ma petite soeur Caroline

c. _____ mon oncle Édouard

d. _____ ma tante Alice

e. _____ moi

f. _____ mon papa

g. _____ ma mère

Nom _____

Classe _____ Date _____

Discovering
FRENCH *Nouveau!*

BLEU

Unité 5
Leçon 16
Video Activities

🌐 **16.4 Activité 5.** Un immeuble à Paris   Counter 24:28–25:47

A. Before you watch the **Vignette culturelle**, answer the following question.

Question personnelle: Have you lived in or visited an apartment building? If so, what features did it have (elevator, security system, number of floors, etc.)?

Réponse: _____

_____

B. Now watch the **Vignette culturelle** and decide whether each statement below is true (**vrai**) or false (**faux**). Circle the appropriate word.

1. Many people who work in the Paris area prefer to live in the city.   **vrai   faux**

2. The **Quartier Saint-Germain** is on the left bank.   **vrai   faux**

3. The buildings in the **Quartier Saint-Germain** are three or four stories high.   **vrai   faux**

4. Most buildings in the **Quartier Saint-Germain** are modern.   **vrai   faux**

5. Main entrances of apartment buildings are protected by a secret code.   **vrai   faux**

6. The **interphone** is a type of intercom system.   **vrai   faux**

C. Question personnelle: If you lived in a French metropolitan area, would you prefer to live in the city or the suburbs? Why?

Réponse: _____

_____

Nom _____

Classe _____ Date _____

Discovering
FRENCH
Nouveau!

BLEU

Activité 6. Votre famille

You and a partner each make a list of six names of relatives (or neighbors and friends). Then you share your lists. Take turns asking and answering questions about the relationship you each have to the people on your lists. Follow the model.

▶ ÉLÈVE 1: **Beth Wilson. Qui est-ce?**
　ÉLÈVE 2: **C'est ma tante.**

Beth Wilson
_____

_____

_____

_____

_____

_____

MODULE 16 Où habitez-vous?

Video 3, DVD 2
Counter 20:35–21:27

*Where do you live? In a large city? In the suburbs? In a small town? Most French people who live in big cities live in apartments. Often there are shops on the first floor, which is called **le rez-de-chaussée**. Some buildings are modern. Others are old. In the suburbs, apartment buildings are more modern and often grouped in high-rise complexes. Of course, many people live in individual houses of varying styles.*

16.1 Presentation: Listening—C'est ma maison
Counter 21:28–22:29

This is Nathalie Aubin's house. Let's say hello.

NATHALIE: Eh bien voilà. C'est ma maison.
Et ça, c'est la maison des voisins. C'est leur maison.
Ça, c'est notre voiture. Et ça, c'est leur voiture.
Voici ma mobylette.
Et voilà la mobylette de mon frère. C'est sa mobylette.
Voici notre living.
Voici ma chambre.
Et voici la chambre de mes parents. C'est leur chambre.
Voici la chambre de ma soeur. C'est sa chambre.

16.2 Mini-scenes: Listening—C'est ta voiture?
Counter 22:30–23:27

Now let's see how people talk about things they own.

—C'est ta voiture?
—Eh bien, oui, c'est ma voiture.

—C'est votre voiture?
—Euh oui, c'est ma voiture.

—C'est ton stylo?
—Non, ce n'est pas mon stylo!

—C'est ton ordinateur?
—Ben, oui . . . c'est mon ordinateur. Tu veux jouer avec moi?

—Ouais!

—C'est votre maison?
—Oui, c'est ma maison.

—C'est notre maison.

—C'est mon sandwich!
—Non, ce n'est pas ton sandwich. C'est mon sandwich!
—Mais non, ce n'est pas votre sandwich. C'est mon sandwich!

—C'est ton copain?
—Non, c'est le copain de ma cousine.
—Ah, bon, dommage!

16.3 Dialogue: C'est ta famille?
Counter 23:28–24:27

Today Valérie is visiting Olivier. She notices some old family pictures. Listen.

VALÉRIE: C'est ta famille?
OLIVIER: Oui, c'est ma famille.
VALÉRIE: Qui est-ce?
OLIVIER: C'est ma grand-mère.
VALÉRIE: Et ça, c'est ton grand-père?
OLIVIER: Non, pas du tout. C'est mon oncle Édouard.
VALÉRIE: Et le petit garçon, qui est-ce?
OLIVIER: Eh bien, c'est moi.
VALÉRIE: Vraiment? Quel âge as-tu sur la photo?
OLIVIER: Quatre ans.
VALÉRIE: Et les grandes personnes, qui est-ce?
OLIVIER: Eh bien, voilà mon papa, et voici ma mère. Et voici ma tante Alice et son mari, et leurs enfants.
VALÉRIE: Et la petite fille qui joue dans l'eau?
OLIVIER: C'est ma petite soeur Caroline.
CAROLINE: Salut!
VALÉRIE: Qui est-ce?
OLIVIER: Eh bien, c'est ma petite soeur Caroline.

16.4 Vignette culturelle: Un immeuble à Paris
Counter 24:28–25:47

Many people who work in the Paris area prefer to live in the city itself rather than in the suburbs. Here we are in the Quartier Saint-Germain, *a middle class area on the left bank. The buildings are six or seven stories high. Most of the buildings are relatively old, but they are well built and quite comfortable. Let's go into this building with Pierre, who's visiting a friend. To open the main door, you have to push a button. At night, when the front door is locked, you have to punch in the secret code of the building.*

Once you're in the building, you ring the bell of the person you are going to visit. Then you identify yourself on the **interphone.**

—Oui.
—Allô, c'est moi, Pierre.
—D'accord. J'ouvre

Many older buildings in Paris don't have elevators, so you have to walk up the stairs. This is very good for your legs and your heart!

Now we've reached the **quatrième étage** *where Pierre's friend lives.*

—Bonjour.
—Bonjour, ça va?
—Oui, ça va. Entre.

IMAGES   À Paris

C.1 Introduction à Paris
Counter 26:10–27:23

Bonjour! *For many people, French and foreign visitors alike, Paris is the most beautiful city in the world. Today, we are going to visit Paris with a young Frenchman who lives there. We're even going to take a boat trip.*

Let's look at a map of Paris. Paris is located on the Seine River, which divides the city into two parts:

- *the right bank,* **la rive droite,** *to the north, and*
- *the left bank,* **la rive gauche,** *to the south.*

Paris has many monuments and places of interest. In our visit, we will see **le Sacré Coeur, Notre Dame, la tour Eiffel, les Champs-Élysées, le Quartier latin, le Louvre, le Centre Pompidou, le musée d'Orsay** *and* **la Villette.** *Now, let's meet our guide.*

C.2 Interview avec Jean-Marc Lacoste
Counter 27:24–28:15

ISABELLE: Bonjour! Comment est-ce que tu t'appelles?
JEAN-MARC: Jean-Marc Lacoste.
ISABELLE: Tu habites à Paris?
JEAN-MARC: Oui, j'habite dans le Quartier latin.
ISABELLE: À quelle école est-ce que tu vas?
JEAN-MARC: Je vais à l'école Alsacienne.
ISABELLE: Comment est-ce que tu vas là-bas?
JEAN-MARC: Ça dépend. Souvent je vais à pied. J'adore marcher.
ISABELLE: Qu'est-ce que tu fais le week-end?
JEAN-MARC: J'aime sortir avec mes copains.
ISABELLE: Qu'est-ce que vous faites?
JEAN-MARC: Ça dépend. On va au Centre Pompidou. On va aussi au Louvre. Ou bien, on reste dans le Quartier latin. On va au cinéma . . . on va dans les boutiques . . . on va au café . . . il y a le choix ici.
ISABELLE: Est-ce que tu veux me faire visiter Paris?
JEAN-MARC: Mais oui, bien sûr.
ISABELLE: Bon. Alors, allons-y!

C.3 Visite de Paris

Counter 28:16–32:22

JEAN-MARC: Voici la tour Eiffel. Elle a 300 mètres de haut. Elle a été construite en 1889 par l'ingénieur Gustave Eiffel. D'ici, on a une très belle vue sur Paris. Là, c'est la Seine. À gauche, c'est l'Arc de Triomphe. Là-bas, c'est le Sacré Coeur. À droite, c'est Notre Dame. Et là-bas, c'est le Centre Pompidou.
Ici nous sommes sur les Champs-Élysées. C'est la plus grande avenue de Paris. En haut, c'est l'Arc de Triomphe.
Ici nous sommes au Quartier latin. C'est le quartier des étudiants. Ce quartier est toujours très animé. Il y a beaucoup de cafés, de restaurants et de librairies. Voici le Marché aux Fleurs. Est-ce que tu aimes ces fleurs? Regarde là-bas. C'est Notre Dame, la cathédrale de Paris. Voilà le musée d'Orsay. C'est le nouveau musée de Paris. Autrefois, c'était une gare. Ici nous sommes au Louvre. Autrefois, c'était une résidence royale. Maintenant, c'est un musée. Regarde cette pyramide de verre. Elle a été construite par un architecte américain. Ici nous sommes devant le Centre Pompidou. C'est un musée d'art moderne. Tu aimes cette architecture?

ISABELLE: Qui, j'aime assez, mais beaucoup de gens n'aiment pas ça.

JEAN-MARC: Je viens souvent ici avec mes copains. Il y a toujours beaucoup d'animation. Est-ce que tu aimes ces sculptures flottantes? Moi, j'adore ça. Regarde cette bouche! Ici nous sommes au parc de la Villette. Cette sphère géante s'appelle la Géode. À l'intérieur, il y a un Omni cinéma. Ici c'est la Cité des sciences et de l'industrie. C'est un musée scientifique. Là-bas, c'est le Zénith où les grandes vedettes de la musique viennent donner des concerts.
Ici nous sommes à l'extérieur de Paris, dans la banlieue ouest. Ce quartier s'appelle la Défense. C'est un quartier d'affaires. Il y a aussi un très grand centre commercial avec des magasins, des cinémas, des restaurants … en hiver, il y a une patinoire! Maintenant, c'est une salle d'exposition.

C.4 Promenade en bateau-mouche

Counter 32:23–34:19

ISABELLE: Tu veux faire une promenade en bateau mouche?

JEAN-MARC: D'accord!

During the boat ride, Isabelle and Jean-Marc are going up the Seine to the east and then returning. Their boat will go under several bridges, pass along the quais, and then circle an island named Île de la Cité, "Island of the City." It is on this tiny island that Paris was founded more than 2,000 years ago. On the Île de la Cité stands Notre Dame, one of the most famous cathedrals in the world. But hurry! The boat is leaving.

URB
p. 131

LEÇON 16 Mes voisins

PE AUDIO

CD 3, Track 14
Compréhension orale, p. 226

Mes voisins

Bonjour!

Je m'appelle Frédéric Mallet.

J'habite à Paris avec ma famille.

Nous habitons dans un immeuble de
six étages.

Voici mon immeuble et voici mes voisins.

Monsieur Lacroche habite au sixième étage
avec sa femme. Ils sont musiciens. Lui, il
joue du piano et elle, elle chante. Oh là là,
quelle musique!

Mademoiselle Jolivet habite au cinquième
étage avec son oncle et sa tante.

Paul, mon meilleur ami, habite au quatrième
étage avec sa soeur et ses parents.

Mademoiselle Ménard habite au troisième
étage avec son chien Pomme, ses deux chats
Fritz et Arthur, son perroquet Coco et son
canari Froufrou. (Je pense que c'est une
personne très intéressante, mais mon père
pense qu'elle est un peu bizarre.)

Monsieur et Madame Boutin habitent au
deuxième étage avec leur fils et leurs
deux filles.

Et qui habite au premier étage?

C'est un garçon super-intelligent, super-
cool et très sympathique! Et ce garçon . . .
c'est moi!

CD 3, Track 15
Écoutez et répétez., p. 226

You will now hear a paused version of the
dialog. Listen to the speaker and repeat right
after he or she has completed the sentence.

CD 3, Track 16
Vocabulaire: La famille, p. 229

Écoutez et répétez.

Repeat the names of the family members
after the speaker.

la famille #

les grands-parents #
le grand-père #la grand-mère #

les parents #
le père # la mère
le mari # la femme

les enfants
un enfant # une enfant
le frère # la soeur #
le fils # la fille #

les parents
l'oncle # la tante
le cousin # la cousine

Prononciation, p. 233

CD 3, Track 17

Les voyelles /o/ et /ɔ/

Écoutez: vélo   téléphone

The French vowel /o/ is pronounced with
more tension than in English. It is usually
the last sound in a word.

Répétez: /o/ #   vélo # radio # nos # vos #
eau # château # chaud #
Nos vélos sont au château. #

The French vowel /ɔ/ occurs in the middle of
a word. Imitate the model carefully.

Répétez: /ɔ/ #   téléphone # école # Nicole #
notre # votre # copain #
prof # dommage #
Comment s'appelle votre
prof? #

À votre tour!

CD 3, Track 18

1. Allô!, p. 234

Listen to the phone conversation. *Écoutez la conversation entre Émilie et Bernard.*

ÉMILIE: Avec qui est-ce que tu vas au cinéma?

BERNARD: Avec mon copain Marc.

ÉMILIE: C'est le cousin de Monique?

BERNARD: Non, c'est son frère.

ÉMILIE: Tu connais leurs parents?

BERNARD: Bien sûr, ils sont très sympathiques.

ÉMILIE: Ils sont canadiens, n'est-ce pas?

BERNARD: Non, mais leurs voisins sont de Québec.

CD 3, Track 19

2. Créa-dialogue, p. 234

Listen to the sample *Créa-dialogues.* *Écoutez les conversations.*

Modèle: —C'est le vélo de Paul?
—Non, ce n'est pas son vélo.
—Tu es sûr?
—Mais oui. Son vélo est bleu.

Maintenant, écoutez le dialogue numéro 1.

—C'est la guitare d'Alice?
—Non, ce n'est pas sa guitare.
—Tu es sûr?
—Mais oui. Sa guitare est brune.

WORKBOOK AUDIO

Section 1. La famille

CD 9, Track 25

A. Écoutez et répétez., p. 137

Repeat the names of the family members after the speaker.

la famille		
les grands-parents	le grand-père	
	la grand-mère	
les parents	le père	la mère
le mari	la femme	
les enfants	un enfant	une enfant
le frère	la soeur	
le fils	la fille	
des parents	l'oncle	la tante
	le cousin	
	la cousine	

CD 9, Track 26

B. Compréhension orale, p. 137

Today, Valérie is visiting Olivier. She notices some old family pictures, which you can see in your workbook. Listen to what Olivier says and make the correct identifications by writing the number of the picture next to the corresponding name.

VALÉRIE: C'est ta famille?

OLIVIER: Oui, c'est ma famille.

1. VALÉRIE: Qui est-ce?
   OLIVIER: C'est ma grand-mère. #

2. VALÉRIE: Et ça, c'est ton grand-père?
   OLIVIER: Non, pas du tout! C'est mon oncle Édouard. #

3. VALÉRIE: Et le petit garçon? Qui est-ce?
   OLIVIER: Eh bien, c'est moi. #

4. VALÉRIE: Et les grandes personnes, qui est-ce?
   OLIVIER: Eh bien, voilà mon papa, et voici ma mère. Et voici ma tante Alice et son mari et leurs enfants. #

Now check your answers. You should have matched the pictures with the people as follows: a-1, b-4, c-4, d-4, e-2, f-4, g-4, and h-3.

CD 9, Track 27

C. Questions et réponses, p. 138

Look at Frédéric's family tree in your Workbook. Someone will ask you questions about various people. Say how they are related to Frédéric. If you are not sure of the answer, listen to the confirmation and then repeat the statement.

Modèle: Qui est Éric Vidal?
(*response*) C'est le cousin de Frédéric.

Qui est François Mallet? #
C'est le père de Frédéric. #

Qui est Suzanne Mallet? #
C'est la grand-mère de Frédéric. #

Qui est Isabelle Vidal? #
C'est la tante de Frédéric. #

Qui est Catherine Vidal? #
C'est la cousine de Frédéric. #

Qui est Véronique Mallet? #
C'est la soeur de Frédéric. #

Qui est Maurice Vidal? #
C'est l'oncle de Frédéric. #

Qui est Albert Mallet? #
C'est le grand-père de Frédéric. #

Qui est Martine Mallet? #
C'est la mère de Frédéric. #

Section 2. Les adjectifs possessifs

CD 9, Track 28

D. Écoutez et répétez., p. 138

Repeat the following nouns with their corresponding possessive adjectives.

mon copain, ma copine, mes amis #

ton père, ta soeur, tes parents #

son baladeur, sa chaîne hi-fi, ses CD #

notre maison, nos voisins #

votre école, vos profs #

leur tante, leurs cousins #

CD 9, Track 29

E. Écoutez et parlez., p. 138

You will hear several items mentioned. Say that each item belongs to you.

Modèle: une guitare # C'est ma guitare. #

Commençons.

un baladeur #	
	C'est mon baladeur.
une chaîne hi-fi #	C'est ma chaîne hi-fi.
des livres #	Ce sont mes livres.
un portable #	C'est mon portable.
des CD #	Ce sont mes CD.

Now say that the following items belong to you and your family.

Modèle: une maison # C'est notre maison.

Commençons.

une voiture #	C'est notre voiture.
un ordinateur #	C'est notre ordinateur.
des photos #	Ce sont nos photos.

CD 9, Track 30

F. Parlez., p. 139

Someone will ask you whether each of the following objects belongs to a specific person. Say that they do.

Modèle: C'est la voiture de Marc? #
Oui, c'est sa voiture.

Commençons.

C'est la voiture de Pauline? # Oui, c'est sa voiture.

C'est le baladeur de Stéphane? # Oui, c'est son baladeur.

C'est le portable de Pierre? # Oui, c'est son portable.

C'est la guitare de Jean-Philippe? # Oui, c'est sa guitare.

Now you will be asked if the following objects belong to several people. Say that they do.

Modèle: C'est la maison de tes voisins? #
 Oui, c'est leur maison.

Commençons.

C'est la maison de tes cousins? #
Oui, c'est leur maison.

C'est la voiture de tes parents? #
Oui, c'est leur voiture.

Ce sont les CD de tes copains? #
Oui, ce sont leurs CD.

Ce sont les photos de tes amis? #
Oui, ce sont leurs photos.

CD 9, Track 31

G. Compréhension orale, p. 139

Now you will hear what certain people are doing with certain objects. Can you determine whether these objects belong to them or to someone else? Listen carefully to the possessive adjective in each sentence. If the object belongs to the person mentioned, check Row A. If the object belongs to someone else, check Row B.

Modèles: J'écoute mes CD. #

I am listening to my CDs. You would check Row A.

Stéphanie regarde mes photos. #

Stéphanie is looking at my photos. You would check Row B.

Commençons.

1. Pauline écoute son baladeur. #
2. Je regarde ton livre. #
3. Vous faites une promenade dans votre voiture. #
4. Thomas mange mon hamburger. #
5. Nous écoutons ta mini-chaîne. #
6. Isabelle regarde mes photos. #

7. Marc fait une promenade avec ton vélo. #
8. Tu téléphones avec ton portable. #
9. J'écoute tes CD. #
10. Charlotte et François jouent avec leurs raquettes. #

Now check your answers. You should have marked Row A for 1, 3, 8, and 10. You should have marked Row B for 2, 4, 5, 6, 7, and 9.

Section 3. Dictée

CD 9, Track 32

H. Écoutez et écrivez., p. 139

You will hear Nathalie showing you around her neighborhood and her house. Listen carefully as she repeats each description and fill in the missing words in your Workbook.

Modèle: Eh bien, voilà. C'est ma maison. #

You would write **ma** in the blank.

Listen again and fill in the missing words.

Commençons.

1. Et ça, c'est la maison des voisins. C'est leur maison. #
2. Ça, c'est notre voiture. Et ça c'est leur voiture. #
3. Voici ma mobylette. #
4. Et voilà la mobylette de mon frère. C'est sa mobylette. #
5. Voici notre cuisine. #
6. Voici ma chambre. #
7. Et voici la chambre de mes parents. C'est leur chambre. #
8. Voici la chambre de ma soeur. C'est sa chambre. #
9. Ah, mais ça, ce n'est pas son baladeur! C'est mon baladeur. #

LESSON 16 QUIZ

Part I: Listening

CD 15, Track 4

A. Questions et réponses

You will hear your French friend Rose ask you six questions. Select the MOST LOGICAL response and circle the corresponding letter (a, b, or c). You will hear each question twice.

Let's begin.

1. *You and Rose are in the parking area in front of your school. She sees a black scooter and asks:*
   C'est le scooter de Jean-Louis?

2. *Now Rose points to a bicycle. She asks:*
   C'est ton vélo?

3. *It is Saturday and you meet Rose at a café. She asks:*
   Où sont tes copines?

4. *You and Rose are walking in your neighborhood. She notices a car and asks:*
   C'est votre voiture?

5. *Rose points down the street. She asks:*
   C'est la maison de tes grands-parents?

6. *Now you and Rose are walking past a tennis court. She asks:*
   Pourquoi est-ce que ton copain ne joue pas au tennis?

7. *Rose wants to know more about your family. You are showing her a photo album. She asks:*
   Ton père a une soeur?

8. *Rose sees another photograph. She asks:*
   Ton oncle a des enfants?

Nom _____

Classe _____ Date _____

Discovering
FRENCH
Nouveau!

BLEU

Unité 5
Leçon 16
Lesson Quiz

QUIZ 16

PART I: LISTENING

A. Questions et réponses (40 points)

You will hear your French friend Rose ask you eight questions. Select the MOST LOGICAL response and circle the corresponding letter (a, b, or c). You will hear each question twice.

1. You and Rose are in the parking area in front of your school. She sees a black scooter.
   You reply:
   a. Oui, c'est mon scooter.
   b. Oui, c'est ton scooter.
   c. Oui, c'est son scooter.

2. Now Rose points to a bicycle.
   You reply:
   a. Oui, c'est leur vélo.
   b. Non, tu n'as pas de vélo.
   c. Non, c'est le vélo de Sophie.

3. It is Saturday and you meet Rose at a café.
   You reply:
   a. Ils ne sont pas ici.
   b. Il est à la bibliothèque.
   c. Elles sont au centre commercial.

4. You and Rose are walking in your neighborhood. She notices a car.
   You reply:
   a. Oui, c'est sa voiture.
   b. Oui, c'est leur voiture.
   c. Non, notre voiture est rouge.

5. Rose points down the street.
   You reply:
   a. Oui, c'est sa maison.
   b. Oui, c'est leur maison.
   c. Non, ce ne sont pas mes grands-parents.

6. Now you and Rose are walking past a tennis court.
   You reply:
   a. Il n'a pas sa raquette.
   b. Il n'a pas leur raquette.
   c. Il n'a pas ta raquette.

7. Rose wants to know more about your family. You are showing her a photo album.
   You reply:
   a. Oui, c'est ma cousine Alice.
   b. Oui, c'est ma tante Véronique.
   c. Non, ce n'est pas elle.

8. Rose sees another photograph.
   You reply:
   a. Oui, il a des cousins.
   b. Oui, il a un fils et deux filles.
   c. Oui, c'est le frère de ma mère.

PART II: WRITING

B. Possessions (24 points)

The following people all have their own things. Complete each sentence with the appropriate POSSESSIVE ADJECTIVE.

▶ Marc a _son_____ vélo.

1. Nous avons _____ livres.

2. Éric et Vincent ont _____ ordinateur.

3. J'ai _____ appareil-photo.

Nom _____

Classe _____ Date _____

Discovering
FRENCH
Nouveau!

BLEU

4. Hélène a _____ portable.

5. Vous avez _____ voiture.

6. Jean-Claude a _____ guitare.

7. Tu as _____ livres.

8. Mes cousins ont _____ chaîne hi-fi.

C. Les mois de l'année (20 points)

What is the sequence of the months of the year? Complete each sentence below with the appropriate ORDINAL number.

▶ Juin est le _sixième_ mois de l'année.

1. Avril est le _____ mois de l'année.

2. Novembre est le _____ mois de l'année.

3. Janvier est le _____ mois de l'année.

4. Septembre est le _____ mois de l'année.

5. Mai est le _____ mois de l'année.

D. Expression personnelle (16 points)

Answer the following questions in French, using complete sentences.

• How many children are there in your family?

_____

• On weekends, do you go to your cousins?

_____

UNITÉ 5
En ville

CULTURAL CONTEXT: City life—the home, the family, and urban activities

---

FUNCTIONS:

- describing your city
- finding your away around
- describing your home and your family
- making plans to do things in town

RELATED THEMES:

- city places and buildings
- urban transportation
- the home
- members of the family
- activities: sports, games, music

 **POUR COMMUNIQUER**   **Communicative Expressions and Thematic Vocabulary**

Nom _____

Classe _____ Date _____

Discovering
FRENCH
Nouveau!

BLEU

UNITÉ 5 Interviews

In this section you will be interviewed by different people who want to get to know you
better. If you wish, you may write the answers to the interview questions in the space
provided.

Interview 1

I am a French journalist
researching an article on
American homes. What can you
tell me about your own home?

• Est-ce que la cuisine est grande ou petite?
• En général, est-ce que vous dînez dans la
  cuisine ou dans la salle à manger.
• De quelle couleur est ta chambre?
• Combien de *(how many)* chambres est-ce qu'il
  y a dans ta maison?

La maison

• _____
• _____
• _____
• _____

Interview 2

Can you tell me a little bit
more about where you live?

• Est-ce que tu habites dans une grande
  ville ou dans une petite ville?
• Est-ce que tu habites dans un appartement
  ou dans une maison?
• Dans quelle rue habites-tu?
• Comment s'appelle le supermarché dans
  ton quartier?

• _____
• _____
• _____
• _____

Nom

Classe _____ Date _____

Discovering
FRENCH *Nouveau!*
BLEU

Unité 5
Resources

Communipak

Interview 3

I will be moving to your town
next year and want to know
more about you and your
school.

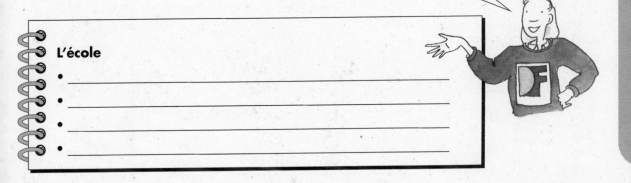

- **Est-ce que tu habites près ou loin de ton école?**
- **Comment est-ce que tu vas à l'école?**
- **À quelle heure est-ce que tu arrives là-bas
  le matin?**
- **À quelle heure est-ce que tu rentres chez toi?**

L'école

- _____
- _____
- _____
- _____

Interview 4

I would like to know what
you and your friends like to
do together.

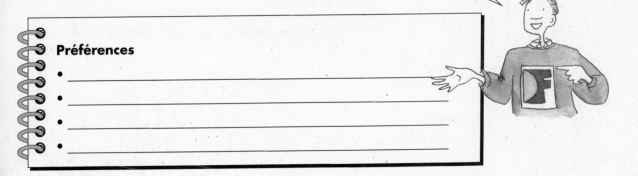

- **Préférez-vous jouer au foot ou au volley?**
- **Préférez-vous faire des promenades à pied
  ou des promenades à vélo?**
- **En général, préférez-vous aller au cinéma ou
  au concert?**
- **En été, préférez-vous aller à la plage ou à
  la piscine?**

Préférences

- _____
- _____
- _____
- _____

Nom _____

Classe _____ Date _____

Interview 5

What we do in our free time often depends on the weather. What are your favorite activities?

1. Qu'est-ce que tu fais quand il fait beau?
2. Qu'est-ce que tu fais quand il neige?
3. Qu'est-ce que tu fais quand il fait froid?
4. Qu'est-ce que tu fais quand il pleut?

Activités

Interview 6

Tell me a little bit about your plans for the weekend.

• Est-ce que tu as un rendez-vous? Si oui, avec qui?
• Où vas-tu aller?
• Qu'est-ce que tu vas faire?
• À quelle heure est-ce que tu vas rentrer chez toi?

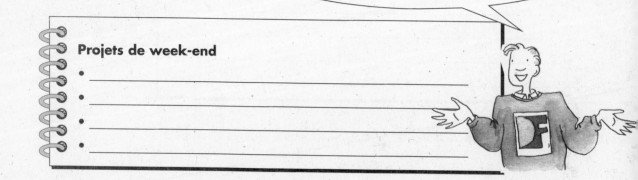

Projets de week-end

Nom _____

Classe _____ Date _____

Discovering
FRENCH
Nouveau!

B L E U

Unité 5
Resources

Communipak

Tu as la parole

Read the instructions on the cards below, and give your partner the corresponding
information in French. Take turns reading your cards and listening to each other.

TU AS LA PAROLE 1 **UNITÉ 5**

Name three places where you and your friends go on
weekends.

▶ **Nous allons . . .**

-
-
-

TU AS LA PAROLE 2 **UNITÉ 5**

Name three rooms in your house and say whether they are
big or small.

▶ **Le salon est assez grand.**

-
-
-

TU AS LA PAROLE 3 **UNITÉ 5**

Choose three professional athletes who play different
sports and say which sport each one plays.

-
-
-

TU AS LA PAROLE 4 **UNITÉ 5**

Describe what you do in your free time. Name . . .

- a team sport that you play
- a game that you play
- a musical instrument that you play (or would like to play)

Nom _____

Classe _____ Date _____

Unité 5 Resources

Communipak

Discovering
FRENCH
Nouveau!

BLEU

TU AS LA PAROLE 5 — UNITÉ 5

Describe your family by saying . . .

- how many brothers you have
- how many sisters you have
- where your grandparents live

TU AS LA PAROLE 6 — UNITÉ 5

Describe your family by saying . . .

- how many uncles you have
- how many aunts you have
- where your cousins live

TU AS LA PAROLE 7 — UNITÉ 5

Name three activities from the following list that you are going to do this weekend.

- go for a walk
- call a friend
- play volleyball
- watch TV
- go for a ride
- go to the movies
- play checkers
- stay home
- play video games

TU AS LA PAROLE 8 — UNITÉ 5

Name two activities from the following list that you are going to do this summer and one activity that you are NOT going to do.

- swim
- play tennis
- go for bike rides
- travel
- visit Paris
- work
- study
- go to school
- speak French

Nom _____

Classe _____ Date _____

Discovering
FRENCH
Nouveau!

BLEU

Side A

Unité 5
Resources

Communipak

Conversations

Act out the following situations with your partner. Take turns:

- In the odd-numbered situations, you will be asking the questions.
- In the even-numbered situations, you will be answering your partner's questions.

CONVERSATION 1   UNITÉ 5

You are new in town and are talking to one of your neighbors (your partner!).

◆————————————————————◆

Ask your partner . . .

- if there is a good restaurant nearby **(près d'ici)**
- if there is a movie theater in the neighborhood
- if there is a swimming pool

CONVERSATION 2

You are a new student in school. You have just invited your partner to your house for the afternoon.

Answer your partner's questions.

CONVERSATION 3   UNITÉ 5

You would like to form a rock group and are looking for musicians.

◆————————————————————◆

Ask your partner . . .

- what instrument **(de quel instrument)** he/she plays
- if he/she plays the guitar
- if he/she plays the drums
- if he/she plays the keyboard

CONVERSATION 4

Your partner has invited you to visit this weekend and is wondering what you would like to do.

Answer your partner's questions.

Nom _____

Classe _____ Date _____

Conversations

Side B

Act out the following situations with your partner. Take turns:

- In the odd-numbered situations, you will be answering your partner's questions.
- In the even-numbered situations, you will be asking the questions.

CONVERSATION 1

Your partner has just moved in next door to you and wants to know some things about the neighborhood.

Answer your partner's questions.

CONVERSATION 2	UNITÉ 5

A new student has invited you to his/her house for the afternoon.

◆━━━━━━━━━━━━━━━━━━━━━━━━━━━━━━━━━━◆

Ask your partner ...

- if he/she lives in the neighborhood
- on which street (**dans quelle rue**) he/she lives
- if he/she lives in a house or an apartment

CONVERSATION 3

Your partner would like to form a rock group and is looking for musicians.

Answer your partner's questions.

CONVERSATION 4	UNITÉ 5

You have invited your friend to visit you this weekend, but are not quite sure what he/she likes to do.

◆━━━━━━━━━━━━━━━━━━━━━━━━━━━━━━━━━━◆

Ask your partner . . .

- if he/she plays ping-pong
- if he/she plays chess
- if he/she wants to go for a bike ride (and if so, where)

Nom _____

Classe _____ Date _____

Discovering
FRENCH *Nouveau!*

BLEU

Side A

Unité 5
Resources

Communipak

Conversations

CONVERSATION 5   **UNITÉ 5**

You want to know what your friends are going to do after class today.

◆————————————————————◆

Ask your partner . . .

- if he/she is going to go to the library
- if he/she is going to go for a walk with his/her friends
- at what time he/she is going to go home

CONVERSATION 6

Your partner wants to know what you are going to do tonight.

Answer your partner's questions.

CONVERSATION 7   **UNITÉ 5**

You are discussing your summer plans with your friends.

◆————————————————————◆

Ask your partner . . .

- if he/she is going to travel (and if so, where he/she is going to go)
- if he/she is going to go to his/her cousins'
- if he/she is going to go to his/her grandparents'

CONVERSATION 8

Today is a holiday. The weather is warm and sunny. Your partner wonders what you are going to do.

Answer your partner's questions.

Conversations

CONVERSATION 5

Your partner wants to know what you are going to do after class today.

Answer your partner's questions.

CONVERSATION 6	**UNITÉ 5**

You want to know what your friends are going to do tonight.

◆━━━━━━━━━━━━━━━━━━━━━━━━━━━━━━◆

Ask your partner . . .

- at what time he/she is going to have dinner
- if he/she is going to watch TV (and if so, which program: **quelle émission?**)
- when he/she is going to study

CONVERSATION 7

You and your partner are discussing summer plans.

Answer your partner's questions about your summer.

CONVERSATION 8	**UNITÉ 5**

Today is a holiday. The weather is warm and sunny.

◆━━━━━━━━━━━━━━━━━━━━━━━━━━━━━━◆

Ask your partner ...

- if he/she is going to stay home
- if he/she wants to go to the beach
- if he/she wants to have a picnic

Nom _____

Classe _____ Date _____

Échanges

1 You want to know how your classmates get to school. You decide to take a poll to find out.

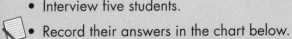

- Interview five students.
- Record their answers in the chart below.

Thomas, comment vas-tu à l'école?

Je vais à l'école à vélo.

NOM	TRANSPORTS					autres transports
▶ Thomas		✔				
1						
2						
3						
4						
5						

- Now summarize your findings.

- _____ élèves vont à l'école à pied.
- _____
- _____
- _____
- _____
- _____

Nom _____

Classe _____ Date _____

2 You are preparing an article for a French magazine about what American teenagers do on weekends.

Dis, Claudia, où vas-tu le samedi après-midi?

Je vais au centre commercial.

- Interview six classmates to find out where they go on Saturday afternoons.
- Check the appropriate box(es) in the chart below.
- If your classmates mention a place that is not listed, add it at the bottom of the chart.

ENDROITS	NOMS						
	▶ Claudia	1	2	3	4	5	6
cinéma							
centre commercial	✔						
bibliothèque municipale							
piscine							
restaurant							
café							
musée							
concert							
théâtre							
chez un copain							
chez une copine							

Nom _____

Classe _____ Date _____

Discovering
FRENCH *Nouveau!*

BLEU

Unité 5
Resources

Communipak

3 You are a French journalist working for a sports magazine. Today you are doing research on what the most popular team sports are in the United States.

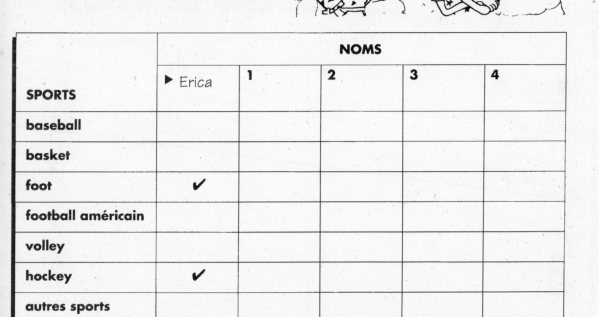

Dis, Erica, quels sports est-ce que tu pratiques?

Je joue au hockey et au foot.

- Ask four classmates which team sports they play. (They may give several answers.)
- Record the answers on the chart.

SPORTS	▶ Erica	1	2	3	4
baseball					
basket					
foot	✔				
football américain					
volley					
hockey	✔				
autres sports					

NOMS

- Now summarize your findings.

- _____ élèves jouent au baseball.
- _____
- _____
- _____
- _____
- _____

Nom _____

Classe _____   Date _____

4 You want to organize a small band.

- Try to find classmates who play at least four of the instruments listed.
- Then ask them each how well they play their instrument.

INSTRUMENT	NOM	Comment joue-t-il? Comment joue-t-elle?				
		très bien	bien	assez bien	comme çi, comme ça	mal
??						

Autres instruments: la trompette, le trombone, la guitare électrique

Nom _____

Classe _____ Date _____

Discovering
FRENCH
Nouveau!

BLEU

Élève A

Tête à tête

1 **Chez les Dupont**

a

There are many people at the Dupont house this weekend. Where is everyone?

 Draw a line connecting each person in the top row to a place you have selected.

■ Your partner will ask you where each of these people is.

Jean-François   **Mme Dupont**   **Tante Michèle**   **Annick**

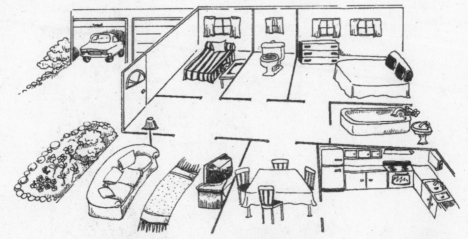

b

Philippe   **M. Dupont**   **Christine**   **Oncle Pierre**

■ Find out from your partner where the people in the bottom row are.

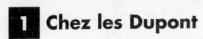 **Où est Philippe?**

 Based on your partner's answer, draw a line connecting each person to the appropriate place.

Nom _____

Classe _____ Date _____

Tête à tête

Élève B

 Chez les Dupont

There are many people at the Dupont house. Where is everyone?

■ Find out from your partner where the people in the top row are.

Où est Jean-François?

Based on your partner's answer, draw a line connecting each person to the appropriate place.

Jean-François   **Mme Dupont**   **Tante Michèle**   **Annick**

Philippe   **M. Dupont**   **Christine**   **Oncle Pierre**

Now you can decide where the people in the bottom row are.

Draw a line connecting each person to the place you have selected.

■ Your partner will ask you where each of these people is.

Unité 5 Resources
Communipak

Nom _____

Classe _____ Date _____

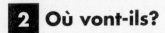

BLEU

Élève A

Unité 5
Resources

Communipak

Tête à tête

2 Où vont-ils?

Look at the map of Belleville. It is a beautiful day and everyone is going out.

 Decide where the people in the top row are going and draw a line connecting each person to an appropriate destination. (Note: Claire is going to the museum.)

■ Your partner will ask you where each one is going.

Claire **Marc et Pierre** **M. Challe** **Mme Rémi** **Anne et Alice**

Isabelle **Julien et Catherine** **Mlle Marty** **M. et Mme Simon** **Nicolas**

■ Find out from your partner where the people in the bottom row are going.

> **Où va Isabelle?**

 Then draw lines connecting each of these people to their corresponding destinations.

Nom _____

Classe _____ Date _____

Tête à tête

Élève B

2 Où vont-ils?

a

Look at the map of Belleville. It is a beautiful day and everyone is going out.

■ Find out from your partner where the people in the top row are going.

> Où va Claire

 Then draw lines connecting each of these people to their corresponding destinations.

| **Claire** | **Marc et Pierre** | **M. Challe** | **Mme Rémi** | **Anne et Alice** |

b

| **Isabelle** | **Julien et Catherine** | **Mlle Marty** | **M. et Mme Simon** | **Nicolas** |

 Decide where the people in the bottom row are going and draw a line connecting each person to an appropriate destination. (Note: Isabelle is going to the theater.)

■ Your partner will ask you where each one is going.

Nom _____

Classe _____ Date _____

Discovering
FRENCH
Nouveau!

BLEU

Unité 5
Resources

Communipak

Élève A

Tête à tête

3 Sports, jeux et musique

a

Look at the following pictures of sports, games, and musical instruments.

 Indicate which ones you play by circling **oui** or **non**.

■ Then answer your partner's questions.

   oui   non

   oui   non

   oui   non

   oui   non

   oui   non

b

■ Now find out which of the following sports, games, and musical instruments your partner plays.

Est-ce que tu joues au tennis?
(Est-ce que tu joues du piano?)

 Indicate your partner's answer by circling **oui** or **non**.

   oui   non

   oui   non

   oui   non

   oui   non

   oui   non

Nom _____

Classe _____ Date _____

Tête à tête

Élève B

3 | Sports, jeux et musique

a

■ Find out which of the following sports, games, and musical instruments your partner plays.

Est-ce que tu joues de la guitare?
(Est-ce que to joues au baseball?)

 Indicate your partner's answer by circling **oui** or **non**.

 oui   non

 oui   non

 oui   non

 oui   non

  oui   non

b

Look at the following pictures of sports, games, and musical instruments.

 Indicate which ones you play by circling **oui** or **non**.

■ Then answer your partner's questions.

  oui   non

 oui   non

 oui   non

 oui   non

 oui   non

Unité 5 Resources
Communipak

Nom _____

Classe _____ Date _____

Discovering FRENCH *Nouveau!*

BLEU

Élève A

Unité 5 Resources Communipak

Tête à tête

4 Deux familles

 a

Your partner is Dominique Blanchet.

■ Find out who the following members of your partner's family are.

Write the answers in the spaces provided.

Qui est Alice Blanchet?

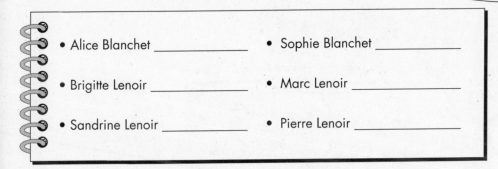

- Alice Blanchet _____
- Sophie Blanchet _____
- Brigitte Lenoir _____
- Marc Lenoir _____
- Sandrine Lenoir _____
- Pierre Lenoir _____

b

Look at the following family tree and imagine that you are Claude Lavie.

■ Your partner will ask you about some members of your family. Tell your partner how they are related to you.

Philippe Lavie? C'est mon père.

Julien Lavie + Marie Lavie

Nicole Lavie + Philippe Lavie   Monique Belcour + Jean-Paul Belcour

Claude Lavie   Marc Lavie   Claire Belcour   Olivier Belcour

URB p. 159

Nom _____

Classe _____ Date _____

Tête à tête

Élève B

4 Deux familles

Look at the following family tree and imagine that you are Dominique Blanchet.

■ Your partner will ask you about some members of your
family. Tell your partner how they are related to you.

Alice Blanchet? C'est ma mère.

Pierre Lenoir + Hélène Lenoir

Brigitte Lenoir + François Lenoir   Alice Blanchet + Paul Blanchet

Sandrine Lenoir   Marc Lenoir   Sophie Blanchet   Dominique Blanchet

· ·

Your partner is Claude Lavie.

■ Find out who the following members of your partner's family are.

  Write the answers in the spaces provided.

Qui est Philippe Lavie?

- Philippe Lavie _____
- Marie Lavie _____

- Olivier Belcour _____
- Jean-Paul Belcour _____

- Monique Belcour _____
- Marc Lavie _____

Nom _____

Classe _____ Date _____

Discovering FRENCH *Nouveau!*

BLEU

Unité 5
Resources

Communipak

Communicative Expressions and Thematic Vocabulary

Pour communiquer
Asking where people are going
Où vas-tu?   *Where are you going?*
    Je vais à + PLACE, EVENT   Je vais au concert.   *I am going to a concert.*
    Je vais chez + PERSON   Je vais chez Pierre.   *I am going to Pierre's house.*
    Je vais chez + STRESS PRONOUN   Je vais chez moi.   *I am going to my house.*

Asking where people are coming from
D'où est-ce que tu viens?   *Where are you coming from?*
Je viens de + PLACE   Je viens de la piscine.   *I am coming from the pool.*

Asking for directions
Excusez-moi, où est [le théâtre]?   Est-ce que c'est | loin?   *Is it* | *far?*
                             | près? | *nearby, close?*

                          Tournez | à gauche.   *Turn* | *to the left.*
                                   | droite. | *to the right.*
                          Continuez tout droit.   *Continue straight ahead.*

Pardon, où sont [les toilettes]:   Elles sont | en haut.   *They are* | *upstairs.*
                                         | en bas | *downstairs.*

Talking about future plans
Qu'est-ce que tu vas faire? Je vais [travailler].   *What are you going to do? I am going to work.*

Expressing possession
C'est mon (ton, son …) livre.   *That's my (your, his, her, …) book.*

Mots et expressions

Moyens de transport *(means of transportation)*
à pied *on foot*   en bus *by bus*   en taxi *by taxi*   en voiture *by car*
à vélo *by bicycle*   en métro *by subway*   en train *by train*

La ville
un boulevard	*boulevard*	une adresse	*address*
un café	*café*	une avenue	*avenue*
un centre commercial	*mall, shopping center*	une bibliothèque	*library*
un cinéma	*movie theater*	une école	*school*
un hôpital	*hospital*	une église	*church*
un hôtel	*hotel*	une piscine	*(swimming) pool*
un magasin	*store*	une plage	*beach*
un musée	*museum*	une rue	*street*
un parc	*park*	une ville	*city, town*
un quartier	*neighborhood*		
un restaurant	*restaurant*		
un stade	*stadium*		
un supermarché	*supermarket*		
un théâtre	*theater*		
un village	*town, village*		

Nom _____

Classe _____ Date _____

La maison

un appartement	*apartment*	une chambre	*bedroom*
un garage	*garage*	une cuisine	*kitchen*
un immeuble	*apartment building*	une maison	*house*
un jardin	*garden, yard*	une salle à manger	*dining room*
un salon	*living room*	une salle de bains	*bathroom*
		les toilettes	*bathroom, toilet*

Quelques endroits où aller

un concert	*concert*	une boum	*party (casual)*
un endroit	*place*	une fête	*party*
un événement	*event*	une soirée	*party (evening)*
un film	*movie*		
un pique-nique	*picnic*		
un rendez-vous	*date, appointment*		

La famille

les parents	*parents; relatives*	la famille	*family*
les grands-parents	*grandparents*		
le grand-père	*grandfather*	la grand-mère	*grandmother*
le père	*father*	la mère	*mother*
le mari	*husband*	la femme	*wife*
un enfant	*child*	une enfant	*child*
le fils	*son*	la fille	*daughter*
le frère	*brother*	la soeur	*sister*
l'oncle	*uncle*	la tante	*aunt*
le cousin	*cousin*	la cousine	*cousin*

Verbes en –er

arriver	*to arrive, to come*
rentrer	*to go back, come back*
rester	*to stay*

jouer à + SPORT, GAME	*to play* *(a sport, game)*
jouer de + INSTRUMENT	*to play* *(an instrument)*

Verbes irréguliers

aller	*to go*
faire une promenade à pied	*to go for a walk*
faire une promenade à vélo	*to go for a bike ride*
faire une promenade en voiture	*to go for a drive*
venir	*to come*
revenir	*to come back*

Les sports

le baseball	*baseball*	le ping-pong	*ping-pong*
le basket(ball)	*basketball*	le tennis	*tennis*
le foot(ball)	*soccer*	le volley(ball)	*volleyball*

Les jeux

les échecs	*chess*	les cartes	*cards*
les jeux d'ordinateur	*computer games*	les dames	*checkers*
les jeux vidéo	*video games*		

Les instruments de musique

le clavier	*keyboard*	la batterie	*drums*
le piano	*piano*	la clarinette	*clarinet*
le saxo(phone)	*saxophone*	la flûte	*flute*
le violon	*violin*	la guitare	*guitar*

Nom _____

Classe _____ Date _____

Discovering
FRENCH *Nouveau!*

BLEU

Unité 5
Resources Communipak

Les nombres ordinaux

premier (première)	*first*	cinquième	*fifth*	neuvième	*ninth*
deuxième	*second*	sixième	*sixth*	dixième	*tenth*
troisième	*third*	septième	*seventh*	onzième	*eleventh*
quatrième	*fourth*	huitième	*eighth*	douzième	*twelfth*

Expressions utiles

Pas du tout!	*Not at all! Definitely not!*	Vas-y!	*Go on!*
Vraiment?!	*Really?!*	Va-t'en!	*Go away!*
Tu es sûr(e)?	*Are you sure?*		

UNITÉ 5 Reading Comprehension

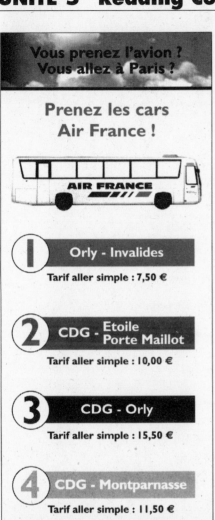

**Vous prenez l'avion ?
Vous allez à Paris ?**

**Prenez les cars
Air France !**

AIR FRANCE

1 Orly - Invalides
Tarif aller simple : 7,50 €

2 CDG - Etoile
Porte Maillot
Tarif aller simple : 10,00 €

3 CDG - Orly
Tarif aller simple : 15,50 €

4 CDG - Montparnasse
Tarif aller simple : 11,50 €

☎ **01 41 56 89 00**
24h/24h, 7/7
Des dépliants sont disponibles à bord des cars Air France.
Leaflets available on board all Air France coaches.

A

Compréhension

1. This is an ad for:
   public transportation   (airport shuttles)

2. How many airports are featured?
   (two)   four

3. What are the airports called?
   CDG, Orly

4. What does **aller simple** mean?
   (one way)   round trip

5. When can you make reservations?
   M-F   M-Sat   (24/7)

Qu'est-ce que vous en pensez?

1. What does **Prenez les cars Air France!** mean?
   Take Air France cars!   (Take Air France buses!)

2. Based on the prices, which airport is closer to Paris?
   Orly

3. Based on the number of shuttles, which airport is bigger?
   CDG

4. Bonus Question: CDG stands for the initials of the most famous 20th Century French politician. Do you know who that is?
   Charles de Gaulle

Nom _____

Classe _____ Date _____

Discovering
FRENCH
Nouveau!

BLEU

carte musées–monuments

Valable 1, 3 ou 5 jours, la carte musées–monuments permet de visiter librement et sans attente 70 musées et monuments de Paris et d'Ile-de-France.

Avantages

– accès libre et prioritaire aux collections permanentes
– nombre de visites illimité
– possibilité d'achat à l'avance

Prix

– carte 1 jour : 15€
– carte 3 jours (consécutifs) : 25€
– carte 5 jours (consécutifs) : 35€

Points de vente à Paris

– musées et monuments participants
– principales stations de métro
– Office de Tourisme de Paris
– magasins FNAC
– escales Batobus

Attention

La carte n'inclut pas l'accès aux expositions temporaires, ni aux visites-conférences. La majorité des musées :
– sont gratuits pour les moins de 18 ans
– accordent des tarifs réduits aux jeunes de 18 à 25 ans
– sont généralement fermés le lundi ou le mardi

Avertissements

Les fermetures et gratuités exceptionnelles (grèves, jours fériés...) qui pourraient intervenir dans les établissements accessibles avec la carte n'entraîneront, ni le prolongement de la durée des cartes, ni le remboursement d'une ou plusieurs journées. Les cartes ne sont ni reprises, ni échangées.

○ Entrée gratuite le premier dimanche de chaque mois.

◖ Entrée gratuite le premier dimanche de chaque mois du 1er octobre au 31 mai inclus.

● Entrée gratuite le dimanche de 10h à 13h.

B

Compréhension

1. What kinds of museum passes are available? Circle all that apply.

   (daily)   2 days   (3 days)   (5 days)   weekly

2. Where are the passes sold? Circle all that apply.

   (at museums and monuments)   in bookstores
   at newspaper stands   (at subway stations)

3. When are the museums generally closed? Circle all that apply.

   (Mon)   (Tue)   Wed   Thu   Fri   Sat   Sun

4. Who has free access to museums and monuments?

   (under 18)   under 25   children

5. Museums marked with a 0 (white circle) are free . . .

   on Sundays   every other Sunday   (the first Sunday of every month)

Qu'est-ce que vous en pensez?

1. What do you think **tarifs réduits** means?

   free entry   (reduced rate)

2. What is an important advantage of having one of these passes?

   (no lining up to buy tickets)   discounts at participating stores

3. Would you need to buy one if you visited Paris this year?

   You do not need a pass if you are under 18.

Nom _____

Classe _____ Date _____

Discovering
FRENCH
Nouveau!

B L E U

Unité 5
Resources
Activités pour tous TE
Reading

MUSÉUM NATIONAL D'HISTOIRE NATURELLE

ZOO DU BOIS DE VINCENNES
- PARC ZOOLOGIQUE DE PARIS -

Le Parc Zoologique de Paris, pour découvrir et partager...

Le Parc Zoologique de Paris vous accueille dans un espace arboré de 15 hectares, et vous présente ses 1200 pensionnaires.

Créé en 1934, à l'issue de l'exposition coloniale de 1931, le Parc Zoologique de Paris s'est transformé au fil des décennies pour devenir un des plus prestigieux parcs zoologiques du monde.

Les nombreuses espèces qui vous y sont présentées figurent, pour certaines, parmi les plus menacées de la planète, pour d'autres, parmi les plus spectaculaires.

Pour assurer leur bien-être et satisfaire 950 000 visiteurs par an, une équipe de 150 personnes oeuvre quotidiennement et s'implique inlassablement dans la protection et la conservation d'espèces.

Rattaché au Muséum National d'Histoire Naturelle, le Parc Zoologique de Paris met en oeuvre de nombreuses missions et s'impose en qualité d'expert en France et partout dans le monde.

Ouvert tous les jours
de 9h à 17h ou 17h30 l'hiver
de 9h à 18h ou 18h30 l'été
Métro Porte Dorée, bus 46, 86, 325.

53, avenue de Saint-Maurice - 75012 PARIS
Tél. : +33 (0)1.44.75.20.00 - Fax : +33 (0)1.43.43.54.73

Tarifs* *Prices*	Adulte	Enfant *(4 à 16 ans)*	Tarif réduit	Groupes scolaires
Entrée	7,62€	4,57€ *gratuit en dessous de 4 ans*	4,57€	1,52€ *par enfant*
Grand Rocher	3,05€	3,05€ *gratuit en dessous de 4 ans*	3,05€	3,05€ *par enfant*

(*) *sous réserve de modification - except modifications*

Consommation annuelle

660 tonnes de fourrage
120 tonnes de céréales
41 tonnes de fruits
92 tonnes de légumes
35 tonnes de viande
30 tonnes de poisson
3700 poulets
9500 oeufs

C

Compréhension

1. How large is the zoo? _15 hectares_

2. How many animals live in the zoo? _1,200 animals_

3. What year did the zoo first open its doors? _1934_

4. How many people visit every year? _950,000 visitors_

5. How many people work there? _150 people_

6. Does the zoo open at the same time every day of the week? _Yes, 9A.M._

Qu'est-ce que vous en pensez?

1. How many tons of food do the animals eat in total per year, not counting chickens and eggs?

nearly 500 tons   (nearly 1,000 tons)   nearly 15,000 tons

2. How many acres does the zoo cover?   (1 hectare = 2.471054 acres)

15 acres   30 acres   (37.5 acres)

URB
p. 167

UNITÉ 5   Reading and Culture Activities

A. En voyage

1. This ad is for . . .
   - ❏ a vacation condo for sale
   - ❏ a house for sale
   - ❏ a house for rent
   - ☑ a small hotel

— *Auberge pasta PIERRE* —

**Cette belle d'autrefois
au coeur du village de Rawdon!**

Salle à manger de 132 places
22 chambres, piscine extérieure
Bar, discothèque, terrasse
Grand salon avec foyer
Forfaits 4 saisons

**3663, rue Queen, Rawdon
J0K 1S0, (514) 834-5417**

2. This concert is going to be held . . .
   - ❏ in a subway station
   - ❏ in a school
   - ❏ in a concert hall
   - ☑ in a church

EGLISE de la MADELEINE
Place et métro Madeleine

Jeudi 29 novembre à 20h 30

MOZART
Concerto pour Clarinette en La M.
REQUIEM

Monique POURADIER DUTEIL, soprano
Sylvie OUSSENKO, mezzo-soprano
Francis BARDOT, ténor
Thierry de GROMARD, basse
Marie-Cécile COURCIER, clarinette
Chœurs de Montmorency
(chef des chœurs : Philippe BRANDEIS)
SINFONIETTA de PARIS
direction : Dominique FANAL

Nom _____

Classe _____ Date _____

3. An attraction of this hotel is that it is located
   - ❏ downtown
   - ☑ near a beach
   - ❏ near an airport
   - ❏ near an amusement park

4. You would go to this place ...
   - ❏ to buy CDs
   - ☑ to read books
   - ❏ to listen to music
   - ❏ to consult bus schedules

5. This map shows you how to get ...
   - ❏ to the downtown area
   - ☑ to a large shopping mall
   - ❏ to a hockey rink
   - ❏ to a racetrack

Nom _____

Classe _____ Date _____

Discovering
FRENCH *Nouveau!*

B L E U

Unité 5
Workbook TE
Reading and Culture Activities
Resources

saint germain

★★★ 10, rue Cassette - 75006 PARIS
Tél. 01 45 44 38 11 - Adresse télég. : Abotel
R.C. Paris B 712 062 744

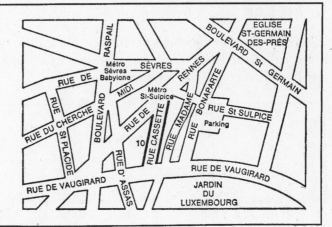

B. À l'hôtel de l'Abbaye

1. You are visiting France with your family and are looking for a hotel.

   • What is the name of the hotel shown on the card? _Hôtel de l'Abbaye_

   • In which city is it located? _Paris_

   • On which street? _rue Cassette_

   • If you wanted to make a reservation, which number would you call? _01.45.44.38.11_

2. You have just made your reservation.

   • Check the address of the hotel and find its location on the map. Mark the location with an "X."

   • You and your family are planning to rent a car while in France. On the map, find and circle the nearest parking garage.

   • Paris has a convenient subway system: **le métro.**

   How many subway stations are shown on the map? _two_

   What is the name of the subway station closest to the hotel? _Métro St-Sulpice_

   • The map shows one of the oldest churches in Paris. (It was built in the 12th century.) Find this church and draw a circle around it.

   What is its name? _St-Germain-des-Prés_

   On which street is it located? _boulevard St-Germain_

   • The map also shows a large public garden where many people go jogging.

   What is the name of the garden? _le jardin du Luxembourg_

   On which street is it located? _rue de Vaugirard_

Nom _____

Classe _____ Date _____

C. En RER

Paris has a regular subway system called **le métro.** It also has a network of fast commuter trains called the **RER** which cross the city in about 12 minutes. If you want to go beyond the city limits, you must pay an extra fare.

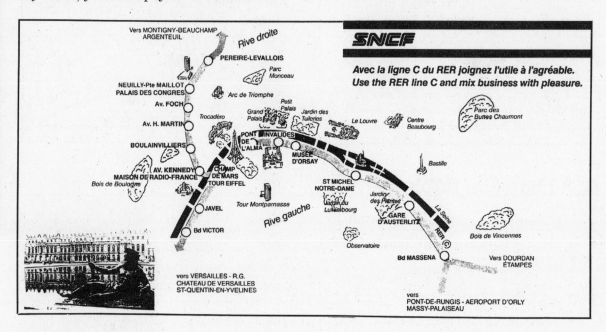

This map shows the C-line of the RER. Many famous monuments and places of interest are located along this line.

1. Look at the map and find at which stop you would get off to visit each of the following places.

   La Tour Eiffel _Champ de Mars/Tour Eiffel/Pont de l'Alma_

   La Cathédrale Notre-Dame _St-Michel/Notre-Dame_

   Le Grand Palais (un musée) _Invalides_

   Le Jardin des Tuileries _Invalides or Musée d'Orsay_

   Le Musée d'Orsay _Musée d'Orsay_

   Le Palais des Congrès _Neuilly-Pte Maillot/Palais des Congrès_

   Le Louvre _Musée d'Orsay_

2. You can also use the C-line to get to places outside of Paris.

   Which airport can you reach with this train? _aéroport d'Orly_

   Which famous historical château can you visit? _Versailles_

Discovering
FRENCH
Nouveau!

BLEU

Unité 5
Resources

Lesson Plan for Images

UNITÉ 5   Images: À Paris, page 246

Objectives

Cultural Goals   To learn about Paris

To recognize major historic and modern attractions

To be aware of various ways of traveling and sightseeing in Paris

Note: You may want to refer back to this Images as attractions and travel in Paris are mentioned in later lessons.

Motivation and Focus

❑ Begin the essay by having students look at the photos and maps on pages 246–253. Encourage them to describe the places and point out landmarks that they have seen before. Encourage students to share any other information they already know about Paris.

❑ As an overview of *À Paris*, play **Video** 3, Tracks C.1–C.4. Replay it, pausing occasionally to allow students to comment on the sights and sounds of the city. Have students identify and locate the places mentioned in the **Video** on the map on page 250.

Presentation and Explanation

❑ To present important facts about Paris, together read page 246. Check understanding by asking questions. Help students pronounce the names of the attractions. Share information in the CULTURE NOTES in the TE margins.

❑ As you present traditional Paris attractions, have students locate them on the map on page 248. Together, read pages 248–249. Guide students to notice the historic and cultural importance of each of the places. Invite students to identify which places they would like to visit. Discuss the CULTURAL BACKGROUND information on pages 248–249 of the TE.

❑ Ask students to contrast the photos of traditional Paris, pages 248–249, with those of new Paris, pages 250–251. What differences in building style and architectural design do they see? Which do they prefer? Read together about *Le nouveau Paris*, helping students with pronunciation and clarifying information as needed. Discuss the CULTURAL BACKGROUND information, page 250 of the TE.

❑ Do the PRE-READING activity, page 252 of the TE, before having students read the letter from Jean-Marc and *Paris en bateau-mouche*, page 253. Check understanding by asking students to summarize the information.

Guided Practice and Checking Understanding

❑ Have students locate the attractions on **Overhead Transparency** 3, Map of Paris. Invite students to briefly describe each of the places. Then do the POST-READING activity on the bottom of page 252 of the TE.

❑ As an alternative, describe each of the attractions and have students identify and locate them on the map of Paris, page 250.

Independent Practice

❑ Arrange students in pairs to work on each *Activité culturelle*, pages 249, 251, and 253. Encourage groups to share their responses with the class.

❑ Students can prepare a list of places they would like to visit with the POST-READING activity, page 252 of the TE. Ask students to explain why they would like to visit the places.

BLEU

Monitoring and Adjusting

❑ As students read the selections, check understanding by having them locate the places on a map of Paris and explain in their own words why these places are famous.
❑ Use **Overhead Transparency** 3 to monitor students' listening skills. Say places and have students find them on the map.

Assessment

❑ As an informal assessment of cultural awareness, replay the **Video** without sound and have students identify the places in Paris.
❑ Have students write their responses to each *Activité culturelle* on pages 249 and 251. Check students' writing for accuracy of cultural information and for supporting their choices.

Reteaching

❑ Use **Overhead Transparency** 3 to reteach sights and attractions of Paris.
❑ To reteach places in Paris, prepare a COMPREHENSION activity. Place pictures of cards with place names around the classroom. Give instructions for students to go to various places.

Extension and Enrichment

❑ Students can prepare a bulletin board display of Paris. Students may want to prepare a large map, drawings of various attractions, and/or brief descriptions of the attractions.
❑ If students are interested, have them research one of the buildings or places mentioned on pages 246–253. Invite students to share their research results with the class.
❑ Students may want to conduct a poll or survey of favorite Paris attractions. Encourage them to make a graph or chart to display the results.

Summary and Closure

❑ Revisit the map in **Overhead Transparency** 3. Guide students to name the important sites and buildings in Paris. Encourage students to share what they have learned about Paris geographically, historically, politically, and economically. Summarize its importance as a capital and as a major city in the world.
❑ Alternatively, replay the **Video** for this essay before summarizing the importance of Paris.

Discovering
FRENCH
Nouveau!

BLEU

Unité 5
Resources

Block Scheduling
Lesson Plan for Images

UNITÉ 5   Images: À Paris, page 246

Block Scheduling (1 day to complete – optional)

Objectives

Cultural Goals   To learn about Paris
To recognize major historic and modern attractions
To be aware of various ways of traveling and sightseeing in Paris

Note: You may want to refer back to this Images as attractions and travel in Paris are mentioned in later lessons.

Block Scheduling

Change of Pace   Make an enlarged photocopy of Overhead Visuals Transparency 3, Map of Paris. Cover the names of the monuments and tape the map on the board. Write the monuments' names on self-adhesive notes and have one student at a time try to place the names correctly on the map in less than one minute.   ■

Day 1

Motivation and Focus

❑ Begin the essay by having students look at the photos and maps on pages 246–253. Encourage them to describe the places and point out landmarks that they have seen before. Encourage students to share any other information they already know about Paris.

❑ As an overview of *À Paris*, play **Video** 3, Tracks C.1–C.4. Replay it, pausing occasionally to allow students to comment on the sights and sounds of the city. Have students identify and locate the places mentioned in the **Video** on the map on page 250.

Presentation and Explanation

❑ To present important facts about Paris, together read page 246. Check understanding by asking questions. Help students pronounce the names of the attractions. Share information in the Culture notes in the TE margins.

❑ As you present traditional Paris attractions, have students locate them on the map on page 248. Together, read pages 248–249. Guide students to notice the historic and cultural importance of each of the places. Invite students to identify which places they would like to visit. Discuss the Cultural background information on pages 248–249 of the TE.

❑ Ask students to contrast the photos of traditional Paris, pages 248–249, with those of new Paris, pages 250–251. What differences in building style and architectural design do they see? Which do they prefer? Read together about *Le nouveau Paris*, helping students with pronunciation and clarifying information as needed. Discuss the Cultural background information, page 250 of the TE.

❑ Do the Pre-reading activity, page 252 of the TE, before having students read the letter from Jean-Marc and *Paris en bateau-mouche*, page 253. Check understanding by asking students to summarize the information.

Guided Practice and Checking Understanding

❑ Have students locate the attractions on **Overhead Transparency** 3, Map of Paris. Invite students to briefly describe each of the places. Then do the Post-reading activity on the bottom of page 252 of the TE.

❑ As an alternative, describe each of the attractions and have students identify and locate them on the map of Paris, page 250.

❑ Have students do the **Block Scheduling Activity** on the previous page.

Independent Practice

❑ Arrange students in pairs to work on each *Activité culturelle*, pages 249, 251, and 253. Encourage groups to share their responses with the class.

❑ Students can prepare a list of places they would like to visit with the POST-READING activity, page 252 of the TE. Ask students to explain why they would like to visit the places.

Monitoring and Adjusting

❑ As students read the selections, check understanding by having them locate the places on a map of Paris and explain in their own words why these places are famous.

❑ Use **Overhead Transparency** 3 to monitor students' listening skills. Say places and have students find them on the map.

Reteaching (as needed)

❑ Use **Overhead Visuals** Transparency 3 to reteach sights and attractions of Paris.

❑ To reteach places in Paris, prepare a COMPREHENSION activity. Place pictures of cards with place names around the classroom. Give instructions for students to go to various places.

Extension and Enrichment (as desired)

❑ Students can prepare a bulletin board display of Paris. Students may want to prepare a large map, drawings of various attractions, and/or brief descriptions of the attractions.

❑ If students are interested, have them research one of the buildings or places mentioned on pages 246–253. Invite students to share their research results with the class.

❑ Students may want to conduct a poll or survey of favorite Paris attractions. Encourage them to make a graph or chart to display the results.

Summary and Closure

❑ Revisit the map in **Overhead Transparency** 3. Guide students to name the important sites and buildings in Paris. Encourage students to share what they have learned about Paris geographically, historically, politically, and economically. Summarize its importance as a capital and as a major city in the world.

❑ Alternatively, replay the **Video** for this essay before summarizing the importance of Paris.

Assessment

❑ As an informal assessment of cultural awareness, replay the **Video** without sound and have students identify the places in Paris.

❑ Have students write their responses to each *Activité culturelle* on pages 249 and 251. Check students' writing for accuracy of cultural information and for support of their choices.

Nom _____

Classe _____ Date _____

Discovering
FRENCH
Nouveau!

BLEU

Unité 5 Resources

Unité 5

Unit Test Form A

UNIT TEST 5 (Lessons 13, 14, 15, 16)

FORM A

Part I: Listening Comprehension

1. The Logical Answer (20 points)

You will hear a series of ten questions. Listen carefully to each question and select the most logical answer on your test sheet. Circle the corresponding letter: a, b, or c. You will hear each question twice.

Modèle: [Où est-ce que vous jouez au foot?]
      a. À l'hôtel.
      b. À l'hôpital.
      c. Au stade.

1. a. À la piscine.
   b. À la bibliothèque.
   c. Rue du Dragon.

2. a. Du cinéma.
   b. Au café.
   c. À midi.

3. a. À pied.
   b. Ça va.
   c. Je vais bien.

4. a. Non, c'est à droite.
   b. Oui, c'est ici.
   c. Merci beaucoup.

5. a. En bas.
   b. Avenue Charles de Gaulle.
   c. Elles sont modernes.

6. a. Oui, il est dans sa chambre.
   b. Non, il est au salon.
   c. Non, il ne mange pas de sandwich.

7. a. Non, ils sont en ville.
   b. Non, ils regardent la télé.
   c. Oui, ils vont rentrer à une heure.

8. a. Je vais nager
   b. Je vais regarder les livres.
   c. Oui, je vais faire une promenade.

9. a. Oui, j'aime bien regarder la télé.
   b. Oui, je reviens du cinéma.
   c. Non, je vais rester chez moi.

10. a. Oui, j'ai un rendez-vous.
   b. C'est loin, n'est-ce pas?
   c. D'accord! Où allons-nous?

Nom _____

Classe _____ Date _____ _____

**Discovering
FRENCH**
Nouveau!

B L E U

Part II. Langauge

2. The Right Place (10 points)

Complete the following sentences with the names of the places listed below. Be logical and do not use the same word more than once.

1. Au complexe sportif où je vais, il y a une _____ olympique.

2. Monsieur Moreau prépare le dîner dans la _____.

3. Nous allons nager à la _____.

4. Le dimanche, beaucoup de personnes vont à l'_____.

5. Les invités *(guests)* dînent dans la _____.

6. Pendant *(during)* la semaine, les enfants vont à l'_____.

7. Il y a beaucoup de livres à la _____.

8. Mon frère aime décorer sa _____ avec des posters.

9. Nous habitons dans un grand _____ de 18 étages *(floors)*.

10. Dans notre _____, il y a des roses et des tulipes.

bibliothèque
chambre
cuisine
école
église
immeuble
jardin
piscine
plage
salle de bains
salle à manger

3. The Right Word (10 points)

For each of the following sentences, select the appropriate completion and write it in the blank.

▶ (de, du)   Où est ma raquette *de*_____ tennis?

1. (de, du)   Les touristes reviennent _____ musée.

2. (à, en)   Samedi, nous allons faire une promenade _____ voiture.

3. (au, à la)   Avec qui est-ce que tu vas _____ théâtre?

4. (à, aux)   Je vais téléphoner _____ cousines de Claire.

5. (à, chez)   Après *(after)* le film, nous allons rentrer _____ nous.

6. (de la, à la)   Est-ce que tu joues _____ guitare?

7. (aux, des)   Alain et Charlotte jouent _____ cartes.

8. (de l', d')   Les élèves rentrent _____ école à midi.

9. (de, d')   Où habitent les cousins _____ Antoine?

10. (de, des)   La maison _____ parents de mon copain est très belle.

Nom _____

Classe _____ Date _____ _____

Discovering
FRENCH
Nouveau!

BLEU

Unité 5
Resources

Unit Test Form A

4. The Right Owner (10 points)

Complete the following sentences with the possessive adjectives that correspond to the underlined subject.

▶ Jean-Pierre écoute *sa* _____ chaîne hi-fi.

1. Nous allons à la boum avec _____ copains.

2. Mes cousins écoutent _____ CD (*pl.*).

3. Est-ce que tu as _____ guitare?

4. Je vais au restaurant avec _____ amie Céline.

5. Vous faites un voyage avec _____ oncle.

6. Charlotte invite _____ copain au restaurant.

7. Est-ce que vous avez _____ cahiers?

8. Les touristes visitent le musée avec _____ guide.

9. Je fais une promenade en ville avec _____ amis.

10. Julie joue au volley avec _____ cousines.

5. The Right Verb (12 points)

Complete the following sentences with the appropriate forms of **aller** or **venir**.

1. À quelle heure est-ce que nous _____ dîner?

2. Le samedi, Mélanie _____ souvent au cinéma.

3. D'où est-ce que vous _____, Madame Koamé?

4. Je n'ai pas faim. Je _____ du restaurant.

5. Pierre et Nathalie _____ regarder la télé chez un copain.

6. Isabelle et Marie-Laure sont canadiennes. Elles _____ de Québec.

Nom _____

Classe _____ Date _____ _____

6. En français, s'il vous plaît! (18 points)

Complete the French equivalents of the English sentences in parentheses.

1. Mes cousins _____.
   (My cousins are at home.)

2. _____ habite à Montréal.
   (Pauline's grandfather lives in Montreal.)

3. Il pleut. Les touristes _____ à l'hôtel.
   (It's raining. The tourists are going to stay at the hotel.)

4. Marc et Julien sont _____.
   (Marc and Julien are at their uncle's house.)

5. Samedi, nous allons _____.
   (Saturday, we are going to go for a drive.)

6. Il y a un supermarché dans la _____.
   (There is a supermarket on Twelfth Avenue.)

Part III. Written Expression

7. Composition (20 points)

Express your personal ideas, using only vocabulary and expressions that you know in French. Write five or six sentences.

Projets

Describe some of the plans you have. Mention what you are going to do (or not going to do) tonight, this weekend, and this summer.

Ce soir *(tonight)*, je _____

_____

_____

_____

Ce week-end, mes amis et moi, nous _____

_____

_____

_____

Cet été *(this summer)*, je _____

_____

_____

_____

Discovering
FRENCH
Nouveau!

BLEU
FORM B

Unité 5
Resources

Unit Test Form B

UNIT TEST 5 (Lessons 13, 14, 15, 16)

Part I. Listening Comprehension

1. The Logical Answer (20 points)

You will hear a series of ten questions. Listen carefully to each question and select the most logical answer on your test sheet. Circle the corresponding letter: a, b, or c. You will hear each question twice.

Modèle: [Où est-ce que vous jouez au foot?]
   a. À l'hôtel.
   b. À l'hôpital.
   c. Au stade.

1. a. À la maison.
   b. Dans une grande ville.
   c. Dans la rue de la République.

2. a. C'est tout droit.
   b. C'est en haut.
   c. C'est en bas.

3. a. Non, c'est loin.
   b. Non, à droite.
   c. Non, c'est près d'ici.

4. a. Oui, ils voyagent.
   b. Oui, ils sont en ville.
   c. Oui, ils sont à la maison.

5. a. Oui, j'habite ici.
   b. Non, je vais dîner chez ma tante.
   c. Non, je reviens à une heure.

6. a. Oui, il est au café.
   b. Oui, il regarde la télé.
   c. Oui, il dîne avec un copain.

7. a. Oui, elle est chez elle.
   b. Oui, elle fait un pique-nique.
   c. Oui, nous allons aller au théâtre.

8. a. Oui, j'étudie beaucoup.
   b. Non, à vélo.
   c. Non, c'est samedi aujourd'hui.

9. a. Oui, c'est ici.
   b. Oui, j'habite en ville.
   c. Non, je vais rester chez moi.

10. a. En métro.
    b. Demain après-midi.
    c. Au centre commercial.

Nom _____

Classe _____ Date _____ _____

Part II. Language

2. The Right Place (10 points)

Complete the following sentences with the names of the places listed below. Be logical and do not use the same word more than once.

1. Le dimanche, les élèves ne vont pas à l'_____.

2. Le réfrigérateur est dans la _____.

3. En été, nous allons en vacances sur une _____ de l'Atlantique.

4. Dans son _____, ma tante cultive des roses.

5. Je dois rendre *(return)* les livres à la _____.

6. Dans ma _____, il y a un lit, un bureau et deux chaises.

7. J'aime nager. En hiver, je nage dans une _____ chauffée *(heated)*.

8. Il y a 20 tables dans la _____ de notre restaurant.

9. L'_____ où mon oncle habite est très moderne.

10. Dans mon quartier, il y a une _____ catholique.

bibliothèque
chambre
cuisine
école
église
immeuble
jardin
piscine
plage
salle de bains
salle à manger

3. The Right Word (10 points)

For each of the following sentences, select the appropriate completion and write it in the blank.

▶ (de, du)   Où est ma raquette *de*_____ tennis?

1. (à, au)   Les athlètes vont _____ stade à huit heures.

2. (à, en)   Dimanche je vais faire une promenade _____ pied.

3. (à, au)   Mes copains sont _____ cinéma.

4. (les, aux)   En classe, le professeur parle _____ élèves.

5. (à, chez)   Après *(after)* la classe, Sophie va rentrer _____ elle.

6. (à la, de la)   Philippe joue _____ clarinette.

7. (aux, des)   Est-ce que vous jouez _____ échecs?

8. (de, du)   Marc revient _____ musée.

9. (de, d')   Comment s'appelle le frère _____ Isabelle?

10. (les, des)   Je n'ai pas l'adresse _____ cousins d'Élodie.

Nom _____

Classe _____ Date _____

Discovering
FRENCH
Nouveau!

BLEU

Unité 5
Resources

Unit Test Form B

4. The Right Owner (10 points)

Complete the following sentences with the possessive adjectives that correspond to the underlined subject.

▶ <u>Jean-Pierre</u> écoute *sa*_____ chaîne hi-fi.

1. Est-ce que <u>vous</u> écoutez toujours _____ professeur?

2. <u>Pauline et Charlotte</u> invitent _____ amis au cinéma.

3. Est-ce que <u>tu</u> vas voyager avec _____ parents?

4. <u>Jérôme</u> est au café avec _____ amie Marie-Claire.

5. <u>Je</u> téléphone à _____ cousine.

6. <u>Vous</u> n'êtes pas toujours d'accord avec _____ amis.

7. <u>Frédéric</u> dîne chez _____ cousins.

8. Est-ce que <u>tu</u> as _____ raquette?

9. <u>Thomas et Claire</u> sont en vacances chez _____ tante.

10. <u>Nous</u> allons redécorer _____ appartement.

5. The Right Verb (12 points)

Complete the following sentences with the appropriate forms of **aller** or **venir**.

1. D'où est-ce que vous _____?

2. Samedi, Pauline et Sophie _____ jouer au basket.

3. Pendant *(during)* les vacances, tu _____ faire un voyage en Chine, n'est-ce pas?

4. Les touristes _____ du musée.

5. Demain nous _____ dîner au restaurant.

6. Patrick est français. Il _____ de la Martinique.

Nom _____

Classe _____ Date _____

6. En français, s'il vous plaît! (18 points)

Complete the French equivalents of the following English sentences.

1. Jérôme _____.
   (Jérôme is not at home.)

2. _____ jouent du piano.
   (Pierre's cousins play the piano.)

3. _____ avec vous.
   (I'm not going to stay with you.)

4. Philippe dîne _____.
   (Philippe is having dinner at a friend's house.)

5. Je voudrais _____ en ville.
   (I would like to go for a walk downtown.)

6. Nous habitons dans la _____.
   (We live on Ninth Avenue.)

Part III. Written Expression

7. Composition (20 points)

Express your personal ideas, using only vocabulary and expressions that you know in French. Write five or six sentences.

Où j'habite

Describe the area where you live, what types of places there are (stores? movie theaters? etc.) and what you do at some of those places.

_____

_____

_____

_____

_____

_____

_____

Nom _____

Classe _____ Date _____

Discovering
FRENCH
Nouveau!

BLEU

Unité 5
Resources

Unité 5 Resources Unit Test Part III

UNIT TEST 5 (Lessons 13, 14, 15, 16)   FORMS A and B

Part III. Cultural Awareness (Alternate)

7. Culture (20 points)

Choose the completion which best reflects the cultural information that you read about in this unit. Circle the corresponding letter: a, b, or c.

1. The population of Paris and its greater metropolitan area is about . . .
   a. 1 million people.   b. 11 million people.   c. 21 million people.

2. Paris, the capital of France, was founded . . .
   a. more than 2000 years ago.   b. in the 10th century.   c. just before the American Revolution.

3. The second-largest city in France is . . .
   a. Lyon.   b. Nice.   c. Tours.

4. In France, streets are often named after . . .
   a. trees.   b. animals.   c. famous people.

5. To see an exhibition of modern art, Parisian young people would go to . . .
   a. **le Centre Pompidou.**   b. **le parc de la Villette.**   c. **l'Arc de Triomphe.**

6. **Les Champs-Élysées** is the name of . . .
   a. a famous discotheque.   b. a French department store chain.   c. a wide avenue in Paris.

7. The most common French pets are . . .
   a. dogs.   b. rabbits.   c. turtles.

8. French is one of the official languages of . . .
   a. The Netherlands.   b. Denmark.   c. Belgium.

9. In a French café, a customer who wants to observe what is going on in the street would sit in the section called . . .
   a. **l'intérieur.**   b. **la terrasse.**   c. **le rez-de-chaussée.**

10. If you were visiting a French friend who lives on **le premier étage** of an apartment building, you would go to . . .
    a. the floor at the street level (corresponding to the American first floor).
    b. the floor above the street level (corresponding to the American second floor).
    c. the top floor.

Nom _____

Classe _____ Date _____

Discovering
FRENCH
Nouveau!

BLEU

UNITÉ 5 Listening Comprehension Performance Test

Partie A. Conversations

This part of the Listening Comprehension Test will let you see how well you understand spoken French. You will hear five short conversations. Look at your Listening Comprehension Test Sheet and read the corresponding questions. After you have heard each conversation the second time, select the correct answer and mark the corresponding letter (a, b, c, or d) on your answer sheet.

1. Listen to the following conversation between a man and a woman.
   Where does the conversation take place?
   a. In a hotel.
   b. In the street.
   c. At the beach.
   d. In a school.

2. Listen to the following conversation between Véronique and Jean-Claude.
   Who is the person in the picture?
   a. Jean-Claude's aunt.
   b. Jean-Claude's mother.
   c. Jean-Claude's cousin.
   d. Jean-Claude's older sister.

3. Listen to the following conversation between Isabelle and Olivier.
   What is Olivier going to do on Sunday?
   a. Go to the movies.
   b. Stay home.
   c. Watch TV.
   d. Visit his cousin Christine.

4. Listen to the following conversation between Frédéric and Caroline.
   Why is Caroline going to the library?
   a. To study.
   b. To pick up a book.
   c. To return a book.
   d. To meet a friend.

5. Listen to the following conversation between Jérôme and his mother.
   What does Jérôme's mother want to know?
   a. Where he is going.
   b. With whom he is going out.
   c. At what time he is coming home.
   d. If he is going to study.

Nom _____

Classe _____ Date _____ _____

Discovering
FRENCH *Nouveau!*

BLEU

Unité 5
Resources

Listening Comprehension
Performance Test

Partie B. Questions et réponses

This part of the Listening Comprehension Test will let you see how well you can handle French questions. You will hear your French friend Olivier ask you five questions. Listen carefully. Then look at your Listening Comprehension Test Sheet and select the MOST LOGICAL answer to the question you heard. Mark the corresponding letter (a, b, c, or d) on your answer sheet. You will hear each question twice.

6. You and Olivier are talking in the school courtyard.
   You reply:
   a. À pied.
   b. À huit heures du matin.
   c. Comme ci, comme ça.
   d. Oui, ça va. Et toi?

7. Olivier meets you and your friends on the street.
   You reply:
   a. D'accord!
   b. Non, nous sommes ici.
   c. Oui, nous jouons au foot.
   d. Oui, nous allons nager.

8. It is Saturday afternoon. You run into Olivier in town.
   You reply:
   a. Oui, je suis en ville.
   b. Oui, je vais étudier à la bibliothèque.
   c. Non, j'habite dans un immeuble.
   d. Non, je vais aller au café avec mes copains.

9. You and Olivier are at your house in the kitchen.
   You reply:
   a. Dans le salon.
   b. En haut à gauche.
   c. Dans dix minutes.
   d. En métro.

10. Olivier is looking out your kitchen window. He notices a car.
    You reply:
    a. Oui, c'est ma voiture.
    b. Non, ce n'est pas sa voiture.
    c. Non, leur voiture est bleue.
    d. Oui, ils font une promenade en voiture.

Discovering
FRENCH
Nouveau!

BLEU

Nom _____

Classe _____ Date _____

UNITÉ 5 Speaking Performance Test

1. Conversations

In this part of the Speaking Performance Test, I will describe a situation and then ask you some related questions. In your answers, use the vocabulary and structures you have learned. Use your imagination.

CONVERSATION A   **UNITÉ 5**

I want to visit your city this summer, so I would like to know some of the places where you go. Please answer my questions.

- Où vas-tu quand tu veux nager?
- Où vas-tu quand to veux dîner en ville?
- Où aimes-tu aller avec tes copains?
- Où aimes-tu aller avec tes parents?

CONVERSATION B   **UNITÉ 5**

I will be attending your school next year, and I want to know more about how you get there. Please answer my questions.

- Est-ce que l'école est loin de ta maison?
- Comment est-ce que tu vas à l'école?
- À quelle heure est-ce que tu arrives là-bas le matin?
- À quelle heure est-ce que tu reviens chez toi?

CONVERSATION C   **UNITÉ 5**

You are all dressed up. I am curious about where you are going.

- As-tu un rendez-vous? Si oui, avec qui?
- Où allez-vous?
- Qu'est-ce que vous allez faire?
- À quelle heure est-ce que tu vas rentrer?

Nom _____

Classe _____ Date _____

Discovering
FRENCH
Nouveau!

B L E U

Unité 5
Resources

Speaking Performance Test

CONVERSATION D   **UNITÉ 5**

I understand your friend Pierre is going out tonight. Tell me
more about his plans.

- Avec qui est-ce qu'il a rendez-vous?
- Où est-ce qu'ils vont aller?
- Qu'est-ce qu'ils vont faire?
- Comment est-ce que Pierre va rentrer chez lui?

CONVERSATION E   **UNITÉ 5**

You are showing me photos of your family. I have some
questions.

- Combien d'enfants est-ce qu'il y a dans ta famille?
- Où habitent tes grands-parents?
- Est-ce que tu as des cousins? Combien?
- Est-ce que tu vas souvent chez tes cousins?

CONVERSATION F   **UNITÉ 5**

Thank you for inviting me to spend a week at your home.
Tell me a little bit more about where you live.

- Est-ce qu'il y a un jardin?
- Est-ce que la cuisine est moderne?
- Combien de chambres est-ce qu'il y a?
- Est-ce que ta chambre est en haut ou en bas?

Nom _____

Classe _____ Date _____

2. Tu as la parole

In this part of the Speaking Test, you have the opportunity to make three comments about a familiar topic. Use only the structures and vocabulary you know. Use your imagination.

TU AS LA PAROLE (A)   **UNITÉ 5**

Name THREE places where you often go. You may use the suggestions below or name other places of your choice.

- the library
- the shopping mall
- the movie theater

TU AS LA PAROLE (B)   **UNITÉ 5**

I know that you like music. Tell me if you play any of the following instruments:

- the piano or the keyboard
- the flute or the clarinet
- the drums or the guitar

TU AS LA PAROLE (C)   **UNITÉ 5**

Tell me THREE things that you are going to do tonight. Use the following activities, or mention other activities of your choice.

- stay home
- go for a walk
- go to a friend's house

Nom _____

Classe _____ Date _____ _____

Discovering
FRENCH
Nouveau!

BLEU

Unité 5
Resources

Speaking Performance Test

TU AS LA PAROLE (D)   UNITÉ 5

I would like to invite you to my place for a week this summer, and would like to know more about what you like to do. Tell me whether or not you like to do THREE of the following things.

- go to the movies
- go to the beach
- play tennis
- play chess
- go on bicycle rides
- play video games

TU AS LA PAROLE (E)   UNITÉ 5

I have a little present for you that I am having delivered to your house. First, I need some directions. Tell me . . .

- do you live in a house or an apartment?
- what street do you live on?
- is your home near the school?

TU AS LA PAROLE (F)   UNITÉ 5

You are visiting Montreal and want to go shopping. I am your Canadian host. Ask me . . .

- if there is a shopping center in the area?
- if it is far?
- if you can go there on foot?

Nom _____

Classe _____ Date _____

UNITÉ 5   Reading Comprehension Performance Test

Read carefully the following ad for a Canadian hotel. Then read the questions. On your Answer Sheet, mark the correct answers by placing a check next to the corresponding letter.

1. What type of hotel is the Hôtel Américain?
   a. A small family-style country inn.
   b. A medium-sized city hotel.
   c. A large resort hotel.

2. According to the ad, what can you find near the hotel?
   a. A public library.
   b. Museums.
   c. An open-air market.

HÔTEL AMÉRICAIN
Pourquoi payer plus cher?

L'Hôtel Américain est situé au coeur du centre-ville, à distance de marche du Vieux-Montréal, du terminus central d'autobus, des restaurants renommés, musées et salles de spectacles. L'Hôtel Américain offre 54 chambres confortables à partir de 35 $ occupation simple, 40 $ occupation double. Prix spéciaux pour groupes. Stationnement gratuit. L'Hôtel Américain, l'endroit "in" où séjourner à Montréal.

1042, RUE SAINT-DENIS, MONTRÉAL (QUÉBEC) H2X 3J2
TÉL : (514) 849-0616

Hôtel Américain

Look carefully at the following announcement. Then read the questions. On your Answer Sheet, mark the correct answers by placing a check next to the corresponding letter.

3. What event is being announced?
   a. A birth.
   b. A wedding.
   c. A school graduation.

4. Where is the event going to take place?
   a. In a reception hall.
   b. At city hall.
   c. In a church.

> *Monsieur et Madame Louis Greiner*
> *ont l'honneur de vous faire part*
> *du mariage de*
> *Monsieur Frank Greiner,*
> *leur fils, avec*
> *Mademoiselle Christine Descroix.*
>
> *Et vous prient d'assister ou de vous unir*
> *d'intention à la messe de mariage qui*
> *sera célébrée le Samedi 24 Août 2003,*
> *à 16 heures 30, en l'Eglise de*
> *Grésy sur Aix (Savoie).*

Nom _____

Classe _____ Date _____

Discovering
FRENCH
Nouveau!

BLEU

Unité 5
Resources

Reading Comprehension
Performance Test

The following map shows part of the downtown area of the French city of Tours. Look at the map and then read the questions. On your Answer Sheet, mark the correct answers by placing a check next to the corresponding letter.

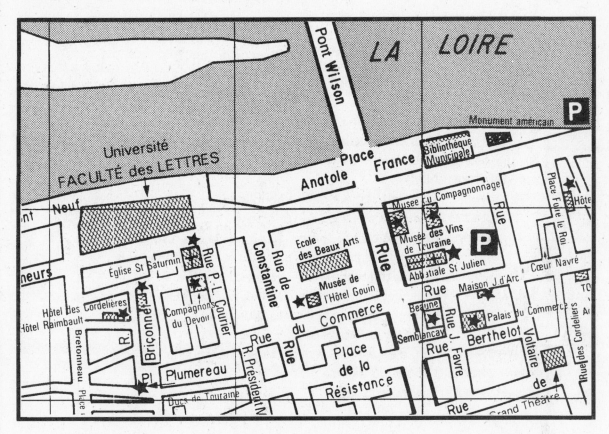

5. According to the map, what place of interest is located on the rue du Commerce?
   a. A church.
   b. A museum.
   c. A post office.

6. If you wanted to borrow a book from the public library, where would you go?
   a. Rue Voltaire.
   b. Place de la Résistance.
   c. Place Anatole France.

7. If you were an art student and wanted to register for classes, where would you go?
   a. Rue de Constantine.
   b. Rue Berthelot.
   c. Pont Wilson.

Discovering
FRENCH
Nouveau!

BLEU

Read the following phone conversation between Philippe and Véronique. Then read the questions. On your Answer Sheet, mark the correct answers by placing a check next to the corresponding letter.

PHILIPPE: Salut, Véronique, ça va?

VÉRONIQUE: Oui, ça va, merci.

PHILIPPE: Dis, est-ce que tu veux venir dîner chez moi samedi soir?

VÉRONIQUE: Oui, je veux bien, merci!

PHILIPPE: Est-ce que tu as mon adresse?

VÉRONIQUE: Non!

PHILIPPE: J'habite 110, rue de la République.

VÉRONIQUE: Comment est-ce qu'on va là-bas?

PHILIPPE: Écoute, c'est très simple. Tu prends le bus jusqu'à l'hôpital Saint Gatien. Tu prends la rue Laënnec et tu tournes à gauche dans l'avenue de la Liberté. Tu continues tout droit sur 200 mètres jusqu'au supermarché. Là, tu tournes à droite et tu es dans la rue de la République.

VÉRONIQUE: Bon, c'est simple. À quel étage est-ce que tu habites?

PHILIPPE: J'habite au sixième.

VÉRONIQUE: Bon alors, à samedi!

8. Which of the following is located near the Hôpital Saint Gatien?
   a. A bus stop.
   b. A subway station.
   c. A supermarket.

9. How should Véronique get from the Hôpital Saint Gatien to Philippe's place?
   a. By bus.
   b. On foot.
   c. By taxi.

10. Where does Philippe live?
    a. Next to a supermarket.
    b. In a small house.
    c. In an apartment building.

Nom _____

Classe _____ Date _____

UNITÉ 5   Writing Performance Test

A. La visite de Michèle (12 points)

Your friend Michèle is going to visit your city next summer. Tell her about the various places in your neighborhood. Mention seven places. Use the list as a guide, or choose your own places.

- a school
- a library
- a swimming pool
- a church
- a shopping center
- stores
- a hospital

Dans mon quartier, il y a . . .

- _____
- _____
- _____
- _____
- _____
- _____
- _____

B. La famille de Vincent (14 points)

Identify the people on the family tree below by indicating their relationships to Vincent. For example, Jacques Lambert is his uncle.

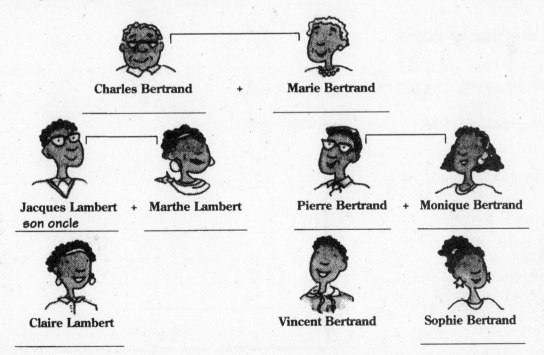

Charles Bertrand   +   Marie Bertrand

Jacques Lambert + Marthe Lambert   Pierre Bertrand + Monique Bertrand
son oncle

Claire Lambert   Vincent Bertrand   Sophie Bertrand

Discovering
FRENCH
Nouveau!

BLEU

Nom _____

Classe _____ Date _____

C. Projets de week-end (20 points)

Indicate whether or not you are going to do the following things this weekend. Use complete sentences.

	Ce week-end
• have dinner in a restaurant	Je _____
• go to a museum	Je _____
• go to a friend's house	Je _____
• stay home	Je _____
• go on a bike ride	Je _____

D. Ce soir (12 points)

The following people all have different plans this evening. In complete sentences, describe what each one is going to do. Use your imagination if necessary.

• Mon copain _____.

• Ma copine _____.

• Les élèves _____.

• Ma famille et moi, nous _____.

E. Voyage à Paris (20 points)

Your aunt Elisabeth, who lives in Paris, has invited you to her house for the month of July. Write a postcard to your friend Jean-Claude to tell him the good news.

In your card, say that . . .

• you are going to go on a trip in July

• you are going to visit Paris

• you are going to stay at your aunt's house

Ask him . . .

• what he is going to do in July

• if he is going to travel too

Sign your card.

Cher Jean-Claude,

_____

_____

_____

_____

_____

_____

_____

Nom _____

Classe _____ Date _____

Discovering
FRENCH
Nouveau!

BLEU

Unité 5
Resources

Writing Performance Test

F. Lettre à Ahmadou (22 points)

Ahmadou, your friend from Senegal, is going to visit you this summer. Write him a short letter describing your home. Answer the questions below.

- Where do you live—in a house or in an apartment?

- How many bedrooms are there?
- How many bathrooms?
- Where is your bedroom—upstairs or downstairs?

- How is your room? big? small? comfortable?

- In which room do you watch TV?
- In which room do you have dinner?

- Is the kitchen modern?
- Is there a garden?

Sign your letter.

Cher Ahmadou,

_____
_____
_____
_____
_____
_____
_____
_____
_____
_____
_____
_____

　　　Amitiés, _____

Discovering
FRENCH
Nouveau!

B L E U

UNITÉ 5   Multiple Choice Test Items

Leçon 13

Look at this address and complete each of the following two statements.

Patrice Lejoyeux
76, avenue Émile Zola
75015 Paris

1. Patrice habite dans _____.
   a. un petit village français
   b. un beau quartier de Montréal
   c. une grande ville

2. —Patrice, quelle est ton adresse?
   —J'habite _____.
   a. c'est une avenue intéressante
   b. à Paris
   c. 76, avenue Émile Zola

3. —Où habites-tu?
   —_____
   a. Montmartre est un joli quartier.
   b. Dans une petite rue derrière le cinéma «Le Paris».
   c. La rue Sainte-Anne est à Québec.

4. Il y a une jolie _____ dans ce quartier.
   a. village
   b. ville
   c. rue

5. Maryse regarde des livres. Il y a des bureaux et des chaises. Des gens travaillent.
   Où est-elle?
   a. à la piscine
   b. à l'église
   c. à la bibliothèque

6. Il fait chaud et j'aime nager. Je voudrais aller à _____.
   a. la plage
   b. l'école
   c. l'église

7. Some hotels have the following.
   a. un restaurant et une piscine
   b. un restaurant et un stade
   c. un café et un supermarché

8. Éliane aime faire des promenades dans _____.
   a. le parc
   b. la piscine
   c. l'école

Nom _____

Classe _____ Date _____ _____

Discovering
FRENCH
Nouveau!

B L E U

Unité 5
Resources

Multiple Choice Test Items

9. Dans _____, il y a des magasins et des gens. Il y a aussi des vélos, des livres, des ordinateurs, etc.
   a. un hôpital
   b. un théâtre
   c. un centre commercial

10. —Où est-ce que tu joues au foot?
    —Au _____.
    a. cinéma, dans ma rue
    b. stade, dans mon quartier
    c. théâtre, dans ma ville

Imagine yourself in a town. The library is on "Church Avenue," on the right side of where you are. The swimming pool is on "Beach Street," left from where you are. The school is on "School Boulevard," on the outskirts of town, quite a distance away. You have to ask for directions. Indicate which of the answers provided is the correct one in each the following three cases.

11. —Pardon monsieur, où est la bibliothèque?
    —_____
    a. Il y a une bibliothèque avenue de l'église.
    b. Il y a une bibliothèque boulevard de la bibliothèque.
    c. Elle est dans la rue de la plage.

12. —Excusez-moi, madame, où est l'école?
    —_____
    a. Tournez à gauche. C'est près.
    b. Elle est boulevard de l'école.
    c. Continuez tout droit. Ce n'est pas loin.

13. —Pardon, mademoiselle, où est la piscine?
    —_____
    a. À droite, mais c'est loin.
    b. C'est à gauche, dans la rue de la plage.
    c. Tout droit, avenue de l'église.

14. —Est-ce que le centre commercial est loin?
    —_____
    a. Oui, il est près.
    b. Non, il est dans la rue Leclerc. C'est près.
    c. Non, il est dans la rue Joffre. La rue Joffre est très loin.

15. —Pour aller au cinéma, tournez _____.
    a. tout droit
    b. c'est à gauche
    c. à droite

16. Dans _____, il y a dix appartements.
    a. mon immeuble
    b. ma maison
    c. mon jardin

Unité 5
Resources

Multiple Choice Test Items

Nom _____

Classe _____ Date _____

Discovering
FRENCH
Nouveau!

B L E U

17. Il y a _____ dans le garage.
    a. le salon
    b. une voiture
    c. une maison

18. Ma chambre est _____, mais la cuisine est en bas.
    a. en haut
    b. dans le jardin
    c. sur la maison

19. Ma famille mange dans _____ en hiver.
    a. la salle de bains
    b. le jardin
    c. la salle à manger

20. If one wants to take a shower, in what room does one go?
    a. les toilettes
    b. la salle de bains
    c. la cuisine

21. One could conceivably wash one's hands in _____.
    a. la salle de bains, la chambre et la salle à manger
    b. la salle de bains, les toilettes et la cuisine
    c. la salle de bains, le salon et le garage

Leçon 14

1. —_____-tu?
   —Très bien, merci!
   a. Ça va
   b. Comment vas
   c. Comment allez

2. Nous aimons nager, alors nous _____ à la piscine.
   a. allons
   b. vont
   c. allez

3. —Brigitte, où est-ce que tu vas?
   —Je _____ à l'école.
   a. allons
   b. va
   c. vais

4. —Maman, papa . . . Où est-ce que vous _____ à midi?
   —Au restaurant!
   a. aller
   b. allez
   c. vont

Nom _____

Classe _____ Date _____ _____

Discovering
FRENCH
Nouveau!

B L E U

Unité 5
Resources

Multiple Choice Test Items

5. —Qui va à Paris?
   —Martin et Pascal _____ à Paris.
   a. allez
   b. vont
   c. allons

6. Roger's pet is behaving badly and is making him angry. What does Roger say?
   a. Va-t'en!
   b. Vas-y!
   c. Allons-y!

7. Michel aime faire des promenades. Dimanche, il va _____ parc.
   a. à
   b. au
   c. aux

8. J'ai soif. Je vais à la _____.
   a. cuisine
   b. café
   c. restaurant

9. J'ai faim. Je voudrais aller _____.
   a. le café
   b. au restaurant
   c. la cuisine

10. Marie fait du foot. Elle va _____.
    a. à la piscine
    b. le parc
    c. au stade

11. —Pardon monsieur, où est l'école?
    —Il faut tourner à droite pour aller _____ école.
    a. à
    b. à l'
    c. à la

12. Le jardin du Luxembourg est _____ super pour faire une promenade.
    a. un événement
    b. à pied
    c. un endroit

13. This afternoon, Chantal is going to a birthday party.
    a. Elle va à une fête.
    b. Elle va à un rendez-vous.
    c. Elle va à une soirée.

14. Jean-Pierre is trying to stay fit.
    Il va au rendez-vous _____.
    a. à pied
    b. en voiture
    c. en métro

Unité 5
Resources

Multiple Choice Test Items

Discovering
FRENCH
Nouveau!

B L E U

Nom _____

Classe _____ Date _____

15. —_____ vas-tu?
   —Chez ma cousine Sylvie.
   a. Comment
   b. Chez qui
   c. Pourquoi

16. Dimanche, je vais _____ grand-père.
   a. au
   b. à mon
   c. chez mon

17. Il y a une boum _____ Françoise, samedi.
   a. chez
   b. à
   c. chez qui

18. —Est-ce que tu vas rentrer chez tes parents samedi?
   —Non, je vais _____ samedi.
   a. rentre
   b. rentrer
   c. rentres

19. —Qu'est-ce que vous _____ à la boum?
   —Nous allons danser!
   a. dansez
   b. n'allez pas
   c. allez faire

20. —Qu'est-ce qu'elles vont faire le 31 décembre?
   —_____
   a. Elles restent à la maison.
   b. Elles vont aller à une soirée.
   c. Elles sont chez un copain.

Leçon 15

1. Ils sont français. Ils _____ de la Martinique.
   a. venir
   b. vient
   c. viennent

2. —Tu reviens à cinq heures?
   —Non, je _____ à sept heures.
   a. revient
   b. reviennent
   c. reviens

3. —_____ vient-il?
   —D'une belle ville en France.
   a. Où
   b. Chez
   c. D'où

Nom _____

Classe _____ Date _____

Discovering
FRENCH
Nouveau!

B L E U

Unité 5
Resources

Multiple Choice Test Items

4. Vous _____ manger au restaurant?
   a. viens
   b. venez
   c. reviennent

5. Il n'a pas soif. Il vient _____ café.
   a. de le
   b. à le
   c. du

6. —Les Galeries Lafayette sont un beau magasin.
   —Oui, je reviens _____ Galeries Lafayette!
   a. à des
   b. aux
   c. des

7. J'ai l'adresse _____ hôpital dans mon cahier.
   a. de la
   b. du
   c. de l'

8. —D'où vient Mélanie? _____ piscine?
   a. Du
   b. De la
   c. À la

9. —Tu joues de la clarinette?
   —Non, non, je joue _____ violon.
   a. du
   b. à la
   c. de la

10. —Je voudrais jouer _____ dames.
    a. aux
    b. du
    c. des

11. —Vous venez avec nous?
    —Oui, je viens avec _____.
    a. moi
    b. toi
    c. vous

12. —Moi, je joue de la guitare, mais _____, ils jouent de la guitare, du violon et du piano!
    a. lui
    b. ils
    c. eux

13. Martine et _____, elles sont copines.
    a. moi
    b. lui
    c. elle

Nom _____

Classe _____ Date _____

14. —Voilà Gérard, n'est-ce pas?
    —Non, ce n'est pas _____.
    a. eux
    b. il
    c. lui

15. —Qui vient à la piscine avec moi?
    —_____!
    a. Je
    b. Tu
    c. Nous

16. —Est-ce que nous allons chez M. et Mme Louvet aujourd'hui?
    —Pas du tout! Nous allons _____ demain.
    a. à eux
    b. d'elles
    c. chez eux

17. How would you answer a friend who tells you she is having dinner with the president?
    a. Pas du tout!
    b. Vraiment!
    c. Dommage!

18. Mon professeur _____ français est super!
    a. de
    b. du
    c. d'

19. —Tu as un livre _____ anglais?
    —Non, mais peut-être à la bibliothèque . . .
    a. de
    b. du
    c. d'

20. Martin cherche un CD _____.
    a. de jazz
    b. du jazz
    c. jazz

Leçon 16

1. C'est le scooter _____.
   a. de Patrick
   b. Patrick
   c. son

2. Le _____ ma mère est mon grand-père.
   a. père du
   b. père de
   c. frère de la

Nom _____

Classe _____ Date _____ _____

Discovering
FRENCH
Nouveau!

BLEU

3. La fille _____ Henri est ma cousine.
   a. de la
   b. de cousine
   c. de l'oncle

4. Papa est le frère _____ Michèle Beaulieu, ma tante.
   a. de
   b. du
   c. de la

5. —C'est la chambre de grand-mère?
   —Non, non, c'est la chambre _____ enfants.
   a. les
   b. d'
   c. des

6. M. Pascal est le professeur _____ Alain.
   a. de
   b. à
   c. d'

7. —M. et Mme Loubert sont tes parents?
   —Non, ce sont _____ grands-parents.
   a. tes
   b. mon
   c. mes

8. —C'est la voiture de M. Baubien?
   —Oui, c'est _____ voiture.
   a. son
   b. sa
   c. ses

9. —Michelle et Patricia sont les cousines de Fabrice.
   —Tu es sûre? Ce sont _____ cousines?
   a. son
   b. sa
   c. ses

10. —_____ cousins sont sympathiques?
    —Oui, mon cousin et ma cousine sont très gentils.
    a. Mes
    b. Ton
    c. Tes

11. Voici _____ amie Laure.
    a. mon
    b. ma
    c. mes

Nom _____

Classe _____ Date _____ _____

12. C'est la maison de l'oncle et de la tante de Jacqueline.
    C'est _____ maison.
    a. sa
    b. ses
    c. leur

13. Voici les vélos de Brigitte et d'Élise. Ce sont _____ vélos.
    a. ses
    b. leur
    c. leurs

14. —Madame Duvois, voici _____ livres!
    a. votre
    b. vos
    c. tes

15. Mme Marion, _____ professeur de maths, est intéressante.
    a. tes
    b. notre
    c. leurs

16. Je suis la voisine de M. et Mme Papineau. Je suis _____ voisine.
    a. leur
    b. sa
    c. ses

17. quatrième, cinquième, _____
    a. sixième
    b. seizième
    c. onzième

18. L'appartement de Liliane est au deuxième étage. L'appartement de Maryse est sous
    l'appartement de Liliane. Où est l'appartement de Maryse?
    Son appartement est au _____ étage.
    a. troisième
    b. premier
    c. première

19. Le _____ième mois de l'année est le mois de septembre.
    a. neuf
    b. neuv
    c. neu

20. Mardi est le deuxième jour de la semaine. Lundi est _____ jour.
    a. la première
    b. premier
    c. le premier

Nom _____

Classe _____ Date _____

Discovering
FRENCH
Nouveau!

B L E U

Unité 5
Resources

Test Scoring Tools

UNITÉ 5 Listening Comprehension Answer Sheet

A. Conversations

1. a. ___   2. a. ___   3. a. ___   4. a. ___   5. a. ___
   b. ___   b. ___   b. ___   b. ___   b. ___
   c. ___   c. ___   c. ___   c. ___   c. ___
   d. ___   d. ___   d. ___   d. ___   d. ___

B. Questions et réponses

6. a. ___   7. a. ___   8. a. ___   9. a. ___   10. a. ___
   b. ___   b. ___   b. ___   b. ___   b. ___
   c. ___   c. ___   c. ___   c. ___   c. ___
   d. ___   d. ___   d. ___   d. ___   d. ___

UNITÉ 5 Reading Comprehension Answer Sheet

1. a. ___   2. a. ___   3. a. ___   4. a. ___   5. a. ___
   b. ___   b. ___   b. ___   b. ___   b. ___
   c. ___   c. ___   c. ___   c. ___   c. ___

6. a. ___   7. a. ___   8. a. ___   9. a. ___   10. a. ___
   b. ___   b. ___   b. ___   b. ___   b. ___
   c. ___   c. ___   c. ___   c. ___   c. ___

Discovering
FRENCH
Nouveau!

BLEU

FORM A

UNIT TEST 5 (Lessons 13, 14, 15, 16)

Part I. Listening Comprehension

CD 15, Track 5

1. The Logical Answer (20 points)

You will hear a series of ten questions. Listen carefully to each question and select the most logical answer on your test sheet. Circle the corresponding letter: a, b, or c. You will hear each question twice. First listen to the model.

Modèle: Où est-ce vous jouez au foot?
You should have circled the letter **"c"**: **Au stade.**

Let's begin. Écoutez.

Un.   Où est-ce que vous habitez?
Deux.   D'où est-ce que tu viens?
Trois.   Comment est-ce que tu vas à ton école?
Quatre.   C'est à gauche?
Cinq.   Où sont les toilettes, s'il vous plaît?
Six.   Est-ce que ton frère est dans la salle à manger?
Sept.   Est-ce que tes cousins sont chez eux?
Huit.   Qu'est-ce que tu vas faire à la piscine?
Neuf.   Nous allons au cinéma. Est-ce que tu veux venir avec nous?
Dix.   Tu veux faire une promenade avec moi?

UNIT TEST 5 (Lessons 13, 14, 15, 16)   **FORM B**

Part I. Listening Comprehension

CD 15, Track 6

1. The Logical Answer (20 points)

You will hear a series of ten questions. Listen carefully to each question and select the most logical answer on your test sheet. Circle the corresponding letter: a, b, or c. You will hear each question twice. First listen to the model.

Modèle: Où est-ce vous jouez au foot?
You should have circled the letter **"c"**: **Au stade.**

Let's begin. Écoutez.

Un.   Pardon, monsieur, où est la bibliothèque?
Deux.   Pardon, mademoiselle, où est l'avenue Charles de Gaulle?
Trois.   Est-ce que les toilettes sont à gauche?
Quatre.   Tes voisins sont chez eux?
Cinq.   Tu vas rester chez toi demain?
Six.   Est-ce que Jean-Claude est au salon?
Sept.   Tu as un rendez-vous avec ta copine samedi?
Huit.   Est-ce que tu vas à l'école à pied?
Neuf.   Est-ce que tu vas faire une promenade en ville?
Dix.   Comment est-ce que vous allez venir chez nous?

Listening Comprehension Performance Test

CD 15, Track 7

Partie A. Conversations

This part of the Listening Comprehension Test will let you see how well you understand spoken French. You will hear five short conversations. Look at your Listening Comprehension Test Sheet and read the corresponding questions. After you have heard each conversation the second time, select the correct answer and mark the corresponding letter (a, b, c, or d) on your answer sheet.

Let's begin.

1. *Listen to the following conversation between a man and a woman.*

   HOMME: Pardon, madame, où est l'hôtel Saint Victor?
   FEMME: Il est dans la rue Saint Victor, monsieur.
   HOMME: C'est loin?
   FEMME: Non, c'est la deuxième rue à droite.
   HOMME: Merci beaucoup.

2. *Listen to the following conversation between Véronique and Jean-Claude.*

   VÉRONIQUE: Qui est-ce, la dame sur la photo?
   JEAN-CLAUDE: C'est la soeur de mon père.
   VÉRONIQUE: Elle est française?
   JEAN-CLAUDE: Non, elle est canadienne.

3. *Listen to the following conversation between Isabelle and Olivier.*

   ISABELLE: Est-ce que tu vas rester chez toi dimanche?
   OLIVIER: Non, je vais aller en ville avec Christine.
   ISABELLE: Qu'est-ce que vous allez faire?
   OLIVIER: Nous allons aller au cinéma.

4. *Listen to the following conversation between Frédéric and Caroline.*

   FRÉDÉRIC: Salut, Caroline! Où vas-tu?
   CAROLINE: Je vais à la bibliothèque.
   FRÉDÉRIC: Tu vas étudier?
   CAROLINE: Non, j'ai rendez-vous avec Jean-Paul.

5. *Listen to the following conversation between Jérôme and his mother.*

   JÉRÔME: Au revoir, Maman. Je vais chez un copain.
   LA MÈRE: À quelle heure est-ce que tu vas rentrer?
   JÉRÔME: À dix heures.
   LA MÈRE: Bon, d'accord! . . . Au revoir, Jérôme.

CD 15, Track 8

Partie B. Questions et réponses

This part of the Listening Comprehension Test will let you see how well you can handle French questions. You will hear your French friend Olivier ask you five questions. Listen carefully. Then look at your Listening Comprehension Test Sheet and select the MOST LOGICAL answer to the question you heard. Mark the corresponding letter (a, b, c, or d) on your answer sheet. You will hear each question twice.

Let's begin.

6. *You and Olivier are talking in the school courtyard. He asks:*
   Comment vas-tu à l'école?

7. *Olivier meets you and your friends on the street. He asks:*
   Vous allez à la piscine?

8. *It is Saturday afternoon. You run into Olivier in town. He asks:*
   Est-ce que tu rentres chez toi?

9. *You and Olivier are at your house in the kitchen. Olivier asks:*
   Dis, où sont les toilettes?

10. *Olivier is looking out your kitchen window. He notices a car and asks:*
    C'est la voiture de tes voisins?

UNITÉ 5 Answer Key

Video Activities

Module 13: La ville et la maison (Pages 21–26)

Activité 1. Les villes de France
1. Lille	6. Bordeaux
2. Paris	7. Grenoble
3. Strasbourg	8. Toulouse
4. Nantes	9. Marseille
5. Lyon	10. Toulon

Activité 2. La ville de Tours
1. e	6. a
2. j	7. c
3. d	8. b
4. i	9. h
5. f	10. g

Activité 3. Qu'est-ce que c'est?
1. magasin
2. café
3. cinéma
4. piscine
5. hôtel
6. restaurant
7. centre commercial
8. bibliothèque

Activité 4. Pardon. Excusez-moi!
1. à droite
2. pas loin/près
3. à droite
4. à gauche, tout droit, pas loin/près

Activité 5. La maison d'Olivier
a. 2	e. 1
b. 7	f. 6
c. 3	g. 5
d. 4	

Activité 6. Votre maison
Floor plans will vary.

Module 14: Une promenade en ville (Pages 56–61)

Activité 1. En ville
1. b	6. b
2. a	7. b
3. b	8. b
4. a	9. a
5. a	

Activité 2. Où allez-vous?
1. a	4. b
2. a	5. b
3. a	

Activité 3. Où vont-ils?
1. a	4. d
2. b	5. e
3. c	

Activité 4. Qu'est-ce que vous allez faire?
a. 2	d. 1
b. 5	e. 3
c. 4	f. 6

Activité 5. Endroits et activités
1. dîner
2. visiter
3. jouer au foot
4. jouer aux jeux vidéo
5. regarder la télé
6. étudier

Activité 6. Tu vas nager?
1. nager
2. étudier
3. jouer au tennis
4. dîner au restaurant
5. organiser une boum

Activité 7. Où va Julien?
1. c
2. c

Activité 8. Le métro
1. vrai	4. vrai
2. vrai	5. faux
3. vrai	

Question personnelle: *Sample answer:* Yes, because it's less expensive than taking a taxi.

Activité 9. En métro
Dialogues will vary.

Module 15: Sports et musique (Pages 91–94)

Activité 1. Quels sports est-ce que vous pratiquez?
a. 2, 7	d. 5
b. 3	e. 1
c. 4, 6	

Activité 2. Sorties
1. b	4. b
2. b	5. a
3. b	

Activité 3. Est-ce que Paul joue au tennis?
1. d	4. a
2. e	5. c
3. f	6. b

Activité 4. Au conservatoire
Students should have marked all items except c and i.

Activité 5. Interview avec Éric
1. a	4. b
2. a	5. b
3. b	

Activité 6. À la Maison des Jeunes
A. *Sample answer:* the school playing fields, my yard
B.
1. a place to do activities and play sports
2. play tennis, play ping-pong, play an instrument, dance, do arts and crafts
C. *Sample answer:* I would like to go there. I would play soccer.

Activité 7. Un jeu: Activités
Games will vary.

Module 16: Où habitez-vous? (Pages 125–128)

Activité 1. Où habitent les Français?
1. b
2. a
3. b

Activité 2. La maison de Nathalie
a. 2	f. 7
b. 9	g. 5
c. 4	h. 3
d. 1	i. 6
e. 8	

Activité 3. À qui est-ce?
1. ma	5. ma; notre
2. ma	6. ton; votre
3. mon	7. ma
4. mon	

Activité 4. La famille d'Olivier
a. 1	e. 3
b. 7	f. 4
c. 2	g. 5
d. 6	

Activité 5. Un immeuble à Paris
A. *Sample answer:* yes; 8 floors, a security system, an elevator
B.
1. vrai	4. faux
2. vrai	5. vrai
3. faux	6. vrai

C. *Sample answer:* I would prefer to live in the city. There is more to do there than in the suburbs.

Activité 6. Votre famille

Lists will vary.

Lesson Quizzes

Quiz 13

Part I: Listening

A. Questions et réponses (40 points)
1. b	5. b
2. c	6. a
3. a	7. b
4. b	8. a

Part II: Writing

B. Le bon endroit (32 points)
1. le cinéma
2. le théâtre
3. le supermarché
4. le stade (le parc)
5. le magasin (le centre commercial)
6. la bibliothèque
7. l'hôpital
8. le musée

C. En ville (12 points)
1. Continuer tout droit.
2. Tournez à droite.
3. Tournez à gauche.

D. Expression personnelle (16 points)
Sample answers:
- J'habite dans une maison (un immeuble).
- Il y a trois chambres et deux salles de bains.

Quiz 14

Part I: Listening

A. Conversations (30 points)
1. a	4. c
2. c	5. b
3. c	6. b

Part II: Writing

B. Où sont-ils? (18 points)
1. à l'	4. au
2. à la	5. à l'
3. au	6. aux

C. Qu'est-ce qu'ils vont faire? (24 points)
1. allons nager
2. vont jouer au basket
3. allez manger
4. vas danser

D. Expression personnelle (28 points)
Sample answers:
- Je vais aller à l'église.
  Je ne vais pas travailler.
- Je vais voyager.
  Je ne vais pas étudier.

Quiz 15

Part I: Listening

A. Conversations (30 points)
1. b	4. a
2. a	5. a
3. b	

Part II: Writing

B. La boum (16 points)
1. venons
2. viens
3. vient
4. viennent

C. Loisirs (12 points)

BLEU

1. du
2. aux
3. de la
4. au

D. À la maison (18 points)
1. lui   4. nous
2. elle   5. elles
3. moi   6. eux

E. Expression personnelle (24 points)
Sample answers:
- Je reviens chez moi à cinq heures.
- Je joue au basket.
- Je voudrais jouer de la flûte.
- Nous aimons jouer aux jeux vidéo.

Quiz 16

Part I: Listening

A. Questions et réponses (40 points)
1. c   5. b
2. c   6. a
3. c   7. b
4. c   8. b

Part II: Writing

B. Possession (24 points)
1. nos   5. votre
2. leur   6. sa
3. mon   7. tes
4. son   8. leur

C. Les mois de l'année (20 points)
1. quatrième   4. neuvième
2. onzième   5. cinquième
3. premier

D. Expression personnelle (16 points)
Sample answers:
- Nous sommes trois enfants dans notre famille. (Il y a trois enfants dans ma famille.)
- Le week-end, nous allons (nous n'allons pas) chez nos cousins.

Communipak

Interviews

Interview 1
Sample answers:
La cuisine est petite.
En général, nous dînons dans la salle à manger.
Ma chambre est bleue.
Il y a six chambres dans ma maison.

Interview 2
Sample answers:
J'habite dans une petite ville.
J'habite dans une maison.
J'habite dans la rue Wildwood.
Il s'appelle Daisy Foodmart.

Interview 3
Sample answers:
J'habite près de mon école.
Je vais à l'école à pied.
J'arrive là-bas à 8 heures.
Je rentre chez moi à 4 heures.

Interview 4
Sample answers:
Nous préférons jouer au volley.
Nous préférons faire des promenades à vélo.
Nous préférons aller au concert.
Nous préférons aller à la plage.

Interview 5
Sample answers:
1. Quand il neige, je joue aux jeux vidéo.
2. Quand il fait beau, je joue au tennis.
3. Quand il fait froid, je vais à la bibliothèque.
4. Quand il pleut, je vais au cinéma.

Interview 6
Sample answers:
Oui, j'ai un rendez-vous avec ma copine Heather.
Nous allons aller à la plage.
Nous allons nager et jouer au volley.
Je vais rentrer à 9 heures.

Tu as la parole

Tu as la parole 1
Sample answers:
Nous allons à la plage.
Nous allons au cinéma.
Nous allons à la bibliothèque.

Tu as la parole 2
Sample answers:
La cuisine est grande.
Ma chambre est petite.
La chambre de mes parents est grande.

Tu as la parole 3
Sample answers:
Shaquille O'Neal—il joue au basket.
Venus Williams—elle joue au tennis.
Derek Jeter—il joue au baseball.

Tu as la parole 4
Sample answers:
Je joue au volley.
Je joue aux échecs.
Je joue du piano.

Tu as la parole 5
Sample answers:
J'ai un frère.
J'ai deux soeurs.
Mes grands-parents habitent à New York.

Tu as la parole 6
Sample answers:
J'ai trois oncles.
J'ai quatre tantes.
Mes cousins habitent à Columbus.

Tu as la parole 7
Sample answers:
Je vais faire une promenade.
Je vais jouer aux jeux vidéo.
Je vais téléphoner à un copain.

Tu as la parole 8
Sample answers:
Je vais nager et jouer au tennis.
Je ne vais pas aller à l'école.

Conversations Side A

Conversation 1
Est-ce qu'il y a un bon restaurant près d'ici?
Est-ce qu'il y a un cinéma dans le quartier?
Est-ce qu'il y a une piscine?

Conversation 2
Sample answers:
Oui, j'habite dans ce quartier. (Non, je n'habite pas dans ce quartier.)
J'habite dans la rue Broadway.
J'habite dans un appartement.

Conversation 3
De quel instrument est-ce que tu joues?
Est-ce que tu joues de la guitare?
Est-ce que tu joues de la batterie?
Est-ce que tu joues du clavier?

Conversation 4
Sample answers:
Oui, je joue au ping-pong.
Non, je ne joue pas aux échecs.
Oui, je voudrais bien faire une promenade à vélo.
Allons au parc!

Conversations Side B

Conversation 1
Sample answers:
Oui, le restaurant Chez Jacques est dans l'avenue Bonaparte.
Non, il n'y a pas de cinéma dans notre quartier.
Oui, il y a une piscine derrière le lycée.

Conversation 2
Est-ce que tu habites dans ce quartier?
Dans quelle rue habites-tu?
Est-ce que tu habites dans une maison ou dans un appartement?

Conversation 3
Sample answers:
Je joue du piano.
Non, je ne joue pas de la guitare.
Non, je ne joue pas de la batterie.
Oui, je joue du clavier.

Conversation 4
Est-ce que tu joues au ping-pong?
Est-ce que tu joues aux échecs?
Est-ce que tu veux faire une promenade à vélo?
Où est-ce que tu veux aller?

Conversations Side A

Conversation 5
Est-ce que tu vas aller à la bibliothèque?
Est-ce que tu vas faire une promenade avec tes amis?
A quelle heure est-ce que tu vas rentrer chez toi?

Conversation 6
Je vais dîner à six heures.
Je vais regarder «The West Wing».
Je vais étudier avant de dîner.

Conversation 7
Est-ce que tu vas voyager? Où est-ce que tu vas aller?
Est-ce que tu vas aller chez tes cousins?
Est-ce que tu vas aller chez tes grands-parents?

Conversation 8
Sample answers:
Non, je ne vais pas rester à la maison.
Oui, je veux bien aller à la plage.
Oui, je veux bien faire un pique-nique.

Conversations Side B

Conversation 5
Non, je ne vais pas aller à la bibliothèque.
Oui, je vais faire une promenade avec mes amis.
Je vais rentrer chez moi à quatre heures.

Conversation 6

À quelle heure est-ce que tu vas dîner?
Est-ce que tu vas regarder la télé? Si oui, quelle émission?
Quand est-ce que tu vas étudier?

Converation 7

Oui, je vais voyager au Canada.
Non, je ne vais pas aller chez mes cousins.
Oui, je vais aller chez mes grands-parents.

Conversation 8

Est-ce que tu vas rester chez toi?
Est-ce que tu veux aller à la plage?
Est-ce que tu veux faire un pique-nique?

Échanges

Échange 1

Sample answers:
Je vais à l'école à pied.
Je vais à l'école en bus.
Je vais à l'école en voiture.
Je vais à l'école en train.
Je vais à l'école en métro., etc.

Échange 2

Sample answers:
Je vais au cinéma.
Je vais à la bibliothèque municipale.
Je vais à la piscine.
Je vais au restaurant.
Je vais au café.
Je vais au musée.
Je vais au concert.
Je vais au théâtre.
Je vais chez un copain.
Je vais chez une copine., etc.

Échange 3

Sample answers:
Je joue au baseball et au basket.
Je joue au football américain.
Je joue au volley et au tennis., etc.

Échange 4

Est-ce que tu joues du saxo?
. . . de la flûte?
. . . de la clarinette?
. . . du violon?
. . . du clavier?
. . . du piano?
. . . de la batterie?

Tête à tête

Activité 1 Chez les Dupont

Élève A
a. *Sample answers:*
Jean-François est dans le salon.
Mme Dupont est dans sa chambre.
Tante Michèle est dans la cuisine.
Annick est dans la salle à manger.
b. Où est M. Dupont?
Où est Christine?
Où est Oncle Pierre?

Élève B
a. *Sample answers:*
Où est Mme Dupont?
Où est Tante Michèle?
Où est Annick?
b. Philippe est dans la cuisine.
M. Dupont est aussi dans la cuisine.
Christine est dans sa chambre.
Oncle Pierre est dans le salon.

Activité 2 Où vont-ils?

Élève A
a. *Sample answers:*
Claire va au musée.
Marc et Pierre vont au centre commercial.
M. Challe va à la bibliothèque.
Mme Rémi va au restaurant.
Anne et Alice vont au théâtre.
b. Où vont Julien et Catherine?
Où va Mlle Marty?
Où vont M. et Mme Simon?
Où va Nicolas?

Élève B
a. Où vont Marc et Pierre?
Où va M. Challe?
Où va Mme Rémi?
Où vont Anne et Alice?
b. *Sample answers:*
Isabelle va au théâtre.
Julien et Catherine vont au supermarché.
Mlle Marty va au stade.
M. et Mme Simon vont au parc.
Nicolas va au cinéma

Activité 3 Sports, jeux et musique

Élève A
a. Oui, je joue au foot. (Non, je ne joue pas au foot.)
Oui, je joue aux cartes. (Non, je ne joue pas aux cartes.)
Oui, je joue de la guitare. (Non, je ne joue pas de la guitare.)
Oui, je joue au baseball. (Non, je ne joue pas au baseball.)
Oui, je joue de la flûte. (Non, je ne joue pas de la flûte.)
b. Est-ce que tu joues au volley?
. . . de la batterie?
. . . aux échecs?

Élève B
a. Est-ce que tu joues de la flûte?
. . . aux cartes?
. . . au foot?
b. Oui, je joue au volley. (Non je ne joue pas au volley.)
Oui, je joue aux échecs. (Non, je ne joue pas aux échecs.)
Oui, je joue du piano. (Non, je ne joue pas du piano.)
Oui, je joue de la batterie. (Non, je ne joue pas de la batterie.)
Oui, je joue au tennis. (Non, je ne joue pas au tennis.)

Activité 4 Deux familles

Élève A
a. C'est sa mère.
C'est sa tante.
C'est sa cousine.
C'est sa soeur.
C'est son cousin.
C'est son grand-père.
b. Olivier Belcour? C'est mon cousin.
Monique Belcour? C'est ma tante.
Marie Lavie? C'est ma grand-mère.
Jean-Paul Belcour? C'est mon oncle.
Marc Lavie? C'est mon frère.

Élève B
a. Brigitte Lenoir? C'est ma tante.
Sandrine Lenoir? C'est ma cousine.
Sophie Blanchet? C'est ma soeur.
Marc Lenoir? C'est mon cousin.
Pierre Lenoir? C'est mon grand-père.

b. C'est son père.
C'est son cousin.
C'est sa tante.
C'est sa grand-mère.
C'est son oncle.
C'est son frère.

Unit Test 5 (Lessons 13, 14, 15, 16)

Form A

Part I. Listening Comprehension

1. The Logical Answer (20 points)

1. c	6. b
2. a	7. a
3. a	8. a
4. a	9. c
5. a	10. c

Part II. Language

2. The Right Place (10 points)

1. piscine	6. école
2. cuisine	7. bibliothèque
3. plage	8. chambre
4. église	9. immeuble
5. salle à manger	10. jardin

3. The Right Word (10 points)

1. du	6. de la
2. en	7. aux
3. au	8. de l'
4. aux	9. d'
5. chez	10. des

4. The Right Owner (10 points)

1. nos	6. son
2. leurs	7. vos
3. ta	8. leur
4. mon	9. mes
5. votre	10. ses

5. The Right Verb (12 points)
1. allons
2. va
3. venez
4. viens
5. vont
6. viennent

6. En français, s'il vous plaît! (18 points)
1. sont à la maison / sont chez eux
2. Le grand-père de Pauline
3. vont rester
4. chez leur oncle
5. faire une promenade en voiture
6. douzième avenue

Part III. Written Expression

7. Composition (20 points)
Answers will vary.

Form B

Part I. Listening Comprehension

1. The Logical Answer (20 points)

1. c	6. b
2. a	7. c
3. b	8. b
4. c	9. c
5. b	10. a

Part II. Language

2. The Right Place (10 points)

1. école	6. chambre
2. cuisine	7. piscine
3. plage	8. salle à manger
4. jardin	9. immeuble
5. bibliothèque	10. église

Unité 5 Resources

Answer Key

Discovering
FRENCH
Nouveau!

B L E U

3. The Right Word (10 points)

1. au	6. de la
2. à	7. aux
3. au	8. du
4. aux	9. d'
5. chez	10. des

4. The Right Owner (10 points)

1. votre	6. vos
2. leurs	7. ses
3. tes	8. ta
4. son	9. leur
5. ma	10. notre

5. The Right Verb (12 points)

1. venez	4. viennent
2. vont	5. allons
3. vas	6. vient

6. En français, s'il vous plaît! (18 points)

1. n'est pas à la maison / n'est pas chez lui
2. Les cousin(e)s de Pierre
3. Je ne vais pas rester
4. chez un(e) ami(e)
5. faire une promenade
6. neuvième avenue

Part III. Written Expression

7. Composition (20 points)
Answers will vary.

Form A/B (Alternate)

Part III. Cultural Awareness

7. Culture (20 points)

1. a	6. c
2. a	7. a
3. a	8. c
4. c	9. b
5. a	10. b

Listening Comprehension Performance Test

A. Conversations

1. b	4. d
2. a	5. c
3. a	

B. Questions et réponses

6. a	9. b
7. d	10. c
8. d	

Reading Comprehension Performance Test

1. b	6. c
2. b	7. a
3. b	8. a
4. c	9. b
5. b	10. c

Writing Performance Test

Suggested Answers
Please note that the answers provided are only suggested answers. Answers will vary.

A. La visite de Michèle (12 points)

une école
une bibliothèque
une piscine
une église
un centre commercial
des magasins
un hôpital

B. La famille de Vincent (14 points)

Charles Bertrand	son grand-père
Marie Bertrand	sa grand-mère
Jacques Lambert	son oncle
Marthe Lambert	sa tante
Pierre Bertrand	son père
Monique Bertrand	sa mère
Claire Lambert	sa cousine
Vincent Bertrand	
Sophie Bertrand	sa soeur

C. Projets de week-end (20 points)

Je (ne) vais (pas) dîner au restaurant.
Je (ne) vais (pas) aller au musée.
Je (ne) vais (pas) aller chez un(e) ami(e).
Je (ne) vais (pas) rester chez moi.
Je (ne) vais (pas) faire une promenade à vélo.

D. Ce soir (12 points)

Mon copain va téléphoner à sa cousine.
Ma copine va regarder la télé.
Les élèves vont étudier.
Ma famille et mois, nous allons dîner en ville.

E. Voyage à Paris (20 points)

Je vais faire un voyage en juillet.
Je vais visiter Paris.
Je vais rester chez ma tante.
Qu'est-ce que tu vas faire en juillet?
Est-ce que tu vas voyager aussi?
Tom

F. Lettre à Ahmadou (22 points)

Cher Ahmadou,
J'habite dans une maison.
Il y a trois chambres.
Il y a une salle de bains.
Ma chambre est en haut.
Elle est petite, mais confortable.
Nous regardons la télé au salon.
Nous dînons dans la salle à manger.
La cuisine n'est pas très moderne.
Il n'y a pas de jardin.
Cécile

Multiple Choice Test Items

Leçon 13

1. c. une grande ville
2. c. 76, avenue Émile Zola
3. b. Dans une petite rue derrière le cinéma «Le Paris».
4. c. rue
5. c. à la bibliothèque
6. a. la plage
7. a. un restaurant et une piscine
8. a. le parc
9. c. un centre commercial
10. b. stade, dans mon quartier
11. a. Il y a une bibliothèque avenue de l'église.
12. b. Elle est boulevard de l'école.
13. b. C'est à gauche, dans la rue de la plage.
14. b. Non, il est dans la rue Leclerc. C'est près.
15. c. à droite
16. a. mon immeuble
17. b. une voiture
18. a. en haut
19. c. la salle à manger
20. b. la salle de bains
21. b. la salle de bains, les toilettes et la cuisine

Leçon 14

1. b. Comment vas
2. a. allons
3. c. vais
4. b. allez

5. b. vont
6. a. Va-t'en!
7. b. au
8. a. cuisine
9. b. au restaurant
10. c. au stade
11. b. à l'
12. c. un endroit
13. a. Elle va à une fête.
14. a. à pied
15. b. Chez qui
16. c. chez mon
17. a. chez
18. b. rentrer
19. c. allez faire
20. b. Elles vont aller à une soirée.

Leçon 15

1. c. viennent
2. c. reviens
3. c. D'où
4. b. venez
5. c. du
6. c. des
7. c. de l'
8. b. De la
9. a. du
10. a. aux
11. c. vous
12. c. eux
13. c. elle
14. c. lui
15. c. Nous
16. c. chez eux
17. b. Vraiment!
18. a. de
19. c. d'
20. a. de jazz

Leçon 16

1. a. de Patrick
2. b. père de
3. c. de l'oncle
4. a. de
5. c. des
6. c. d'
7. c. mes
8. b. sa
9. c. ses
10. c. Tes
11. a. mon
12. c. leur
13. c. leurs
14. b. vos
15. b. notre
16. a. leur
17. a. sixième
18. b. premier
19. b. neuv
20. c. le premier